Pitman Shorthand Speed Development No. 3

New Era Edition

Based on a selection of the Royal Society of Arts Shorthand Examination Papers 1966–1969

By kind permission of the Society

Compiled by
Douglas Eames, M.A.(Bristol), Dip.Ed., F.R.S.A.

PITMAN

PITMAN PUBLISHING LIMITED
39 Parker Street, London WC2B 5PB

Associated Companies
Copp Clark Pitman, Toronto
Fearon Pitman Publishers Inc, San Francisco
Pitman Publishing Pty Ltd, Melbourne
Pitman Publishing New Zealand Ltd, Wellington

© Sir Isaac Pitman and Sons Limited 1973
Reprinted 1974, 1977, 1978, 1979

Isaac Pitman

Text set in 9/10 pt IBM Press Roman, printed by photolithography
and bound in Great Britain at The Pitman Press, Bath

ISBN 0 273 00057 8

G9–(656:24)

Preface

This book contains, in two forms, some of the shorthand examination material set by the Royal Society of Arts in their Ordinary (Single Subject) Examination for the years 1966–1969 together with some original material. It is printed firstly in longhand counted in tens, and secondly in New Era shorthand. The book is arranged to correspond with the five sound-tapes designed to support it. Cassettes are also available. The purpose of the book is to provide practice material for speed development, and preparation for the examinations of the Royal Society of Arts and other public examinations in shorthand.

For the benefit of those students who are still in the early stages of their study, the phrasing used in the early shorthand pages of this book is of a very elementary nature. It is emphasized, however, that no student should ever be penalized for more advanced phrasing provided that she is following the principles laid down in *The New Phonographic Phrase Book*.

The book may be used in a variety of ways according to the needs of particular students and classes. Listed below are some of the ways in which the longhand may be used.

1. For preliminary reading of the material before it is dictated, for visual comprehension, vocabulary, spelling, punctuation, sentence structure, pronunciation, conventional typographical and typewritten representation, paragraphing, aural comprehension, or dictation preparation.

2. For dictation in short "takes," or at any speed.

3. For proof-reading and checking after a transcription exercise.

4. For preliminary reading with the shorthand in mind. Such matters as vowel indication and vowel insertion, phrasing, less frequent outlines, short form practice, revision of theory, may all come up for consideration at this time.

The shorthand may be used in a number of ways.

1. For preparation for subsequent dictation.

2. For reading practice.

3. For fair copying (penmanship exercises).

4. For copied dictation to develop accuracy at low "consolidation" speed.

5. For checking the shorthand note after dictation.

It will be apparent that the book can be used by itself as a teaching aid with the teacher providing all the necessary dictation. The value of the book is much enhanced, however, if it is used in conjunction with the sound-tapes. They provide the timed dictation and the speed development practice and enable the teacher to guide and assist the students, individually and as a class. The dictation is accurate and exact. It can be repeated as often as is required, and it can be used for testing and assessment. By saving the teacher time and effort, it gives him more opportunity to recognize difficulties in recording the spoken word. If the dictation is given through individual headsets it greatly assists the concentration and effort that is necessary for success in shorthand speed. It is now possible to receive such dictation on small individual headset units which pick up their signal from an induction loop, without the necessity for any wiring. Such a system is completely portable.

Sound-tapes will not, in themselves, make fast shorthand writers but they very materially assist both teacher and student towards the goals of fast writing and fast transcription.

The sound-tapes comprise five 5-inch 900 ft. twin-track sound-tapes to be played at 3¾ inches per second. Each track gives about 45 minutes' dictation, so that a reel contains about 1½ hours of practice material.

Cassettes are also available.

All contain repetition at higher speeds and together embody some of the shorthand examination material of the Royal Society of Arts for the years 1966–1969, with some additional material.

Lesson Notes for a 50-minute Period

Information: Twenty-eight students (ages 16–18) all writing shorthand at 80 words a minute and preparing for a 100 words a minute examination.

Equipment: Output of small tape-recorder fed into a thirty-station wiring system, each student having her own individual headset.

Notes

1. Short "warm-up" dictation at 80 w.a.m. (e.g. an anecdote). (½ min.

2. Passage C, p. 38. Read aloud as far as ". . . but many still remain." What is meant by "historical accident?" Who is the Home Secretary? (5 min.)

3. The shorthand. Concentrate on phrases. Revise theory of final downward L. (5 min.)

4. Switch on tape-recorder. Class records first minute only to ". . . mists of time." Run back; re-dictate; re-write; individually-timed reading back. (4 min.)

5. Turn up shorthand on p. 110. Check number of errors in shorthand. Ask six students: "Tell us one error you made. What should it be?" (6 min.)

6. Read remainder of passage from shorthand to class, sentence by sentence. Individuals repeat each sentence. Time them in words a minute. (8 min.)

7. Back to dictation in three "takes" (a) to ". . . mists of time"; (b) to ". . . of their horses"; (c) to the end. (4 min.)

8. Read back after (a) and (b). (3 min.)

9. Repeat (c) dictation. Change notebooks. Read neighbour's shorthand. (2 min.)

10. Short form and phrase drill on twenty short forms and phrases from the passage. Write first on board and read:

> unusual, ourselves, what, more, those, owners, things, for example, whose, it is true, as well as the, how many, in the same way, of course, at first, when, difficult, trade, who are, will be.

(Three times in changed order. Collect last dictation for assessment.) (5 min.)

11. Use "Many of these regulations are certainly the result of historical accident" as penmanship exercise. Write up. Dictate at 60 w.a.m. (10 sec.) and 120 w.a.m. (5 sec.) alternately, three times. (2 min.)

12. Close books. Write in shorthand five words from passage. Long-hand on board:

> activities supervision abolished restaurants frequently

Vocalize. Check. (3 min.)

13. Dictate first minute of repeat dictation at 120 w.a.m. from the sound-tape. (2 min.)

The publishers gratefully acknowledge the courteous co-operation of the Royal Society of Arts in granting permission for the book, sound-tapes and cassettes to be produced.

Contents

	Long-hand PAGE	Short-hand PAGE
TAPE 1 (*White Leader*) 8 passages at 50 words a minute	1	59
TAPE 1 (*Red Leader*) 8 passages at 60 words a minute	5	64
TAPE 2 (*White Leader*) 8 passages at 80 words a minute	9	71
TAPE 2 (*Red Leader*) 8 passages at 80 words a minute	15	78
TAPE 3 (*White Leader*) 8 passages at 80 words a minute	20	86
TAPE 3 (*Red Leader*) 7 passages at 80 words a minute	25	93
TAPE 4 (*White Leader*) 8 passages at 100 words a minute	30	100
TAPE 4 (*Red Leader*) 9 passages at 100 words a minute	32	108
TAPE 5 (*White Leader*) 8 passages at 120 words a minute	43	117
TAPE 5 (*Red Leader*) 8 passages at 120 words a minute	51	126

All passages are dictated once at the set speed, and again at a speed 20 words a minute faster.

PASSAGE A (Tape 1—White Leader)

R.S.A. 50 words a minute, Summer, 1966 (I)

Dear Sir,

It gives us much pleasure to enclose our / latest booklet in the hope that you may be able / to join one of our cruises next year. It may / seem early to plan so far ahead, but it is / advisable as accommodation was fully booked soon after our previous **/**   50
programme was issued.

As you will see from the enclosed / booklet, the ship we have chartered for our cruises has / room for more than five hundred passengers, but, in order / to ensure complete comfort, four hundred persons only will be / carried. There are spacious decks and a large number of **/** pleasant lounges. There will be a small orches- 100
tra and films / will be shown daily.

All bookings will be accepted at / once, subject to the conditions printed on the enclosed forms. /

We shall be pleased to hear from you at an / early date and to give you our advice.

Yours faithfully, /   150

(Shorthand of this passage is on p. 59)

PASSAGE B (Tape 1—White Leader)

R.S.A. 50 words a minute, Summer, 1966 (II)

The power of thought is the greatest power that man / has at his disposal.

To a great extent, the world / is in its present state as a result of collective / thinking.

Every man is what he is and his life / is what it is largely as the outcome of his **/** thoughts. What we think, we become. What we   50
think builds / up our character or pulls it down, makes us happy / or miserable, successful or unsuccessful. Thinking guides us in the / choice of our friends and can make us liked or / disliked. It is often said that we reap what we **/** sow.   100

There is no limit to the power of thought. / Right thinking means right actions, and, although right thinking does / not enable us to avoid the difficulties and troubles of / life, it does help us to meet them and to / face them with a far better chance of overcoming them. **/**   150

(Shorthand of this passage is on p. 59)

1

PASSAGE C (Tape 1—White Leader)

R.S.A. 50 *words a minute, Autumn,* 1966 (I)

If you look at a modern gas or electric stove / you will find a number of burners used for different / ways of cooking food. The camper may need to grill / or boil on his camp fire and to be suc-
50 cessful / he will need various types of fire for various purposes. / It is just not true that he can simply light / one fire and success-fully grill, boil or roast over it. /

His fires must be differently built using the most suitable / fuel available.

For boiling he will need a quick-burning / fuel whereas for
100 grilling and roasting he will need good / hard woods which are a nuisance to get going but / which give an immense heat and little smoke or flame / and produce what is in fact a bed of red- / hot coals.

In addition, a suitable device must be made / to support the
150 pot or whatever is used for cooking. /

(Shorthand of this passage is on p. 60)

PASSAGE D (Tape 1—White Leader)

R.S.A. 50 *words a minute, Autumn,* 1966 (II)

Dear Parents,

We shall be holding our annual prize-giving / this year at the end of May instead of during / the Winter term. We hope to in-clude the presentation of / school prizes with a special sports event and exhibition of / students' work.
50 This will give parents the opportunity of seeing / the work of their children while at the same time / enjoying a pleasant after-noon in the school playing fields.

Members / of the staff will be available during the afternoon to / talk to you about the progress of your son or / daughter, or to
100 answer any questions you may like to / ask about the school, and I hope to have the / pleasure of meeting as many of you as possible on / this occasion.

Further details of what we hope will prove / a memorable day will be sent to you after the / Christmas holiday.

We wish you a happy Christmas.
150 Yours sincerely, /

(Shorthand of this passage is on p. 61)

PASSAGE E (Tape 1—White Leader)

R.S.A. 50 *words a minute, Easter,* 1967 (I)

Dear Sir,

The four dozen electric blankets which were ordered / from you a month ago were not delivered at the / beginning of this week as promised. When we placed the / order we made it very clear that delivery by the / promised date was most important. If at that time you / had any doubt about your ability to keep   50 your promise / we feel that the proper course would have been to/ inform us.

Unfortunately this is not the first time you / have failed to keep your delivery dates and we have / now reached the stage when we feel compelled to point / out that you cannot expect us   100 to continue business with / you on these lines any longer.

When you receive this / letter we hope you will send the blankets immediately and / take steps to ensure that any future orders we may / place with you are dealt with more promptly.

Yours faithfully, /   150

(*Shorthand of this passage is on p.* 61)

PASSAGE F (Tape 1—White Leader)

R.S.A. 50 *words a minute, Easter,* 1967 (II)

In the case of parcels which do not exceed 2/2 lb. in weight delivery is rendered very simple by / the aid of the Post Office. Parcels can be handed / in at any Post Office for dispatch, but as the / rates payable vary with the weight of the parcel and / not   50 with the distance it has to go, the parcel / post is an expensive form of delivery when parcels do / not have to go far. Moreover, the limit of size / and weight renders the service almost useless to the wholesale / trade which is dealing with large quantities. Registration, however, makes / the parcel post a fairly safe means of   100 transport. Also / the Cash on Delivery system enables sellers to hand their / goods to the Post Office together with instructions as to / what to collect from the addressees before handing over the / parcel. There is a limitation of £50 per parcel. /   150

(*Shorthand of this passage is on p.* 62)

PASSAGE G (Tape 1—White Leader)

R.S.A. 50 *words a minute, Whitsun,* 1967 (I)

Dear Sir,

Thank you for your letter of April 20th. / We are sorry to learn that the consignment of china / tea-sets dispatched from our factory on March 30th was / received in a damaged condition, and that you feel the / reason for this is largely due to bad packing.

50   In **/** view of the delay that is likely to occur if / we send our representative to inspect the damage and await / his report, we propose to accept liability and to replace / the broken pieces without further delay.

Would you therefore kindly / send the damaged items to our
100   factory, carriage forward, together **/** with a list of the pieces involved, and we shall / then arrange for the immediate dispatch of replacements.

We do / assure you that a complaint of this nature is most/ unusual and hope that you will accept our apologies for / any trouble to which you have been put.

150   Yours faithfully, **/**

(*Shorthand of this passage is on p.* 63)

PASSAGE H (Tape 1—White Leader)

R.S.A. 50 *words a minute, Whitsun,* 1967 (II)

None of us can ever pay the debt we owe / to those who lived before us — to the men who / made life easier, and happier and healthier for us all. /

Do we ever think, when looking through the window, that /
50   once there was not a pane of glass in the **/** world? Then a man dug things out of the ground, / mixed them, and, with the help of heat, made glass. / Who was he? We do not know. Nor do we / know the man who found fire, or the man who / discovered iron.
100   We do know, however, of those men of **/** a later age who harnessed power, and made ships, railways / and aeroplanes. We know also of others who worked in / various fields to conquer plague and disease of very many / kinds by discovering new drugs and forms of treatment.
150   Let **/** us never forget the debt we owe to these people. /

(*Shorthand of this passage is on p.* 63)

4

PASSAGE A (Tape 1—Red Leader)

R.S.A. 60 *words a minute, Summer,* 1966 (I)

Dear Madam,

May we draw your attention to our new / book on typewriting which we have just published? It gives / us pleasure to enclose a specimen copy.

The material is / presented in a clear and interesting manner and guidance is / given on every important aspect of the subject.

The book / provides training in keyboard mastery. Correspon-   50 dence of all types is / dealt with step by step and there is a variety / of model letters for practice in this most popular section / of the subject. No aspect of typewriting training has been / neglected and such important matters as copying from manuscript, tabulat- ing / and completing commercial forms are displayed in detail.   100 The final / section of the book consists of a selection of past / examination papers in the three stages and some of the / papers have been fully worked.

We are sure that our / new textbook will be most popular with both teachers and / students.   150

May we look forward to the pleasure of hearing / from you? We assure you that any orders you may / care to place will have our prompt attention.

Yours faithfully, /   180

(*Shorthand of this passage is on p.* 64)

PASSAGE B (Tape 1—Red Leader)

R.S.A. 60 *words a minute, Summer,* 1966 (II)

There are few people who do not love animals and / it has been said that a man who is kind / to animals will seldom treat human beings unkindly.

On the / farm, we meet a variety of animals and all of / them are of use. There are those that are kept / for the work they do   50 and others for the produce / they give. Every wise farmer treats his animals with the / utmost care.

There was a time when the most important / working animal on a farm was that noble creature the / horse, but horses are now becoming fewer and fewer on / farms. They still do splendid   100 work and it is important / they should be given wholesome food and healthy stabling.

Another / lovable animal on the farm is the sheep-dog. These / fine helpers do a wonderful job and it is always / a delight to watch them at work. Their skill is / truly amazing. It is usually two years before a sheep-/dog is fully trained and, although his working life is / only about nine years, he still gives help after that. /

150

180

(*Shorthand of this passage is on p.* 65)

PASSAGE C (Tape 1—Red Leader)

R.S.A. 60 *words a minute, Autumn,* 1966 (I)

At London Airport in normal weather, an average of one / plane a minute arrives or departs with unfailing regularity. When/ night falls the activity continues with the runways ablaze with / light.

Not all planes are British. They come from such / places as Australia, India, and America.

Because of the saving / of time, air travel is being increasingly used for longer / journeys, not only abroad but within the British Isles.

One / drawback is that airports are situated some distance from city / centres. Much of the time saved in the air may / be lost travelling to and from airports. Weather conditions such / as fog can cause delays in arrival or departure. Despite / these drawbacks longer and more frequent business trips are now / made because of the speed and convenience of modern air / travel. The up-to-date business man thinks no more / of travelling across a continent for orders than his grandfather / did of travelling from the north to the south of / England. He may leave the airport in fog or snow / and arrive at his destination hours later in brilliant sunshine. /

50

100

150

180

(*Shorthand of this passage is on p.* 66)

PASSAGE D (Tape 1—Red Leader)

R.S.A. 60 *words a minute, Autumn,* 1966 (II)

Credit transactions in business must be carefully recorded if prompt / and proper payment is to be made. Keeping these records / is the work of the Accounts Department, but in a / large firm this work may be spread over several departments. /

6

The main function of the Accounts Department is the record-ing / of all sales and purchases, and of all receipts and / payments 50
of money. No firm could stay in business long / without efficient arrangements for recording and following-up such transactions. /

Nowadays the use of machinery plays a large part in / speed-ing-up the process of recording account entries.

A machine / operator can enter over one thousand entries in 100
one day / compared with several hundred written by hand.

These machines are / often used for other purposes such as wages and costing. /

Some years ago Accounts Departments were staffed almost completely by / men, but with the introduction of machines and the ever / growing need to use all the resources of the country's / 150
labour force, many women and girls are now employed on / this work and some of them are very well paid. / 180

(Shorthand of this passage is on p. 66)

PASSAGE E (Tape 1—Red Leader)

R.S.A. 60 *words a minute, Easter,* 1967 (I)

In the selection of the site for his shop, the / trader may be guided by the capital at his command. / Because of the very high price demanded he may not / be able to obtain possession of the ideal site. In / most cases a main street is to be preferred, that / 50
is, where the traffic is heaviest and where the shop / would come to the notice of the greatest number of / possible customers during the course of the day. There is / a tendency, nowadays, for a group of shops to be / built in a main thoroughfare in the centre of a / residential estate. Such sites are quite suitable for 100
those traders / who will be content with the business available on the / estate but they are somewhat restricted in their future development. / Generally these shops are those which cater for everyday needs. /

Where opportunities present themselves, a corner site has a further / advantage in that two windows are usually available to 150
a / retailer. Shop windows provide a valuable form of publicity to / the shopkeeper and good window displays will increase his business. / 180

(Shorthand of this passage is on p. 67)

R.S.A. 60 *words a minute, Easter,* 1967 (II)

Did you hear that knock at the front door? If / so, you heard it with your ear. It is really / very odd that the door-knocker, which is not even / inside the house, can have anything to do with your / ear, which is indoors in the sitting-room.

50 The air **/** in the house reaches from the front door to your / ear. The knocker first shook the front door, then the / front door shook the air in the house, and the / air shook the drum inside your ear and so you / heard the knock.

100 What is more, different sounds shake the **/** air in a distinctive way so that you recognize sounds. /

All sounds consist of little shakes or waves, but they / are not like the waves of the sea, for they / go backwards and forwards instead of up and down. Watch / a goods train being shunted in

150 the railway yard. The **/** engine bumps gently into the first wagon, and that bumps / into the next, and so on right along the train. /

180 Sound travels through the air in exactly the same way. /

(*Shorthand of this passage is on p.* 68)

R.S.A. 60 *words a minute, Whitsun,* 1967 (I)

Dear Madam,

In answer to your inquiry of 1st May, / we are pleased to send you a copy of our / illustrated holiday tours programme for the coming season.

As you / will see, we offer a very wide choice of tours, / both

50 in this country and abroad. A special feature is **/** that they are planned to suit all tastes, and costs / vary to meet the pockets of those with limited means / as well as those who can afford rather more luxury. /

Needless to say, as we are already approaching the holiday /

100 season, some of the more popular tours are fully booked **/** and these have been indicated, but there are still a / large number of tours for which we have vacancies at / the time of writing.

If you should decide to go / on any of these holidays it would be desirable to / make an early booking. In this case perhaps you

8

will / kindly complete the application form and return it as soon / 150
as possible, together with the appropriate deposit, so that the /
necessary reservation may be made on your behalf.

Yours faithfully, /   180

(*Shorthand of this passage is on p.* 69)

PASSAGE H (Tape 1—Red Leader)

R.S.A. 60 *words a minute, Whitsun,* 1967 (II)

It is not generally known that the Royal Society of / Arts was
founded a hundred years before the commencement of / the
examinations for which it has now become famous. In / its long
history the Society has concerned itself with many / important
developments, some of which were connected with the Industrial / 50
Revolution.

Among the reforms which the Society helped to bring / about
was the abolition of child chimney sweeps. Until the / end of the
18th century very young boys had to / climb up the inside of
chimneys in order to clean / them. But in the late 18th century
the Society of / Arts offered an award for an invention which   100
would make / this unnecessary. The device which received the
prize was almost / the same as that in use today, namely, a number / of rods connected together, with a brush fixed to the / top.

At the first examination in eighteen fifty-five only / one candi- 150
date offered himself, but from that small beginning the / Royal
Society of Arts examinations have grown to their present / size
with more than half-a-million entries a year. /   180

(*Shorthand of this passage is on p.* 69)

PASSAGE A (Tape 2—White Leader)

R.S.A. 80 *words a minute, Summer,* 1966 (I)

It is a great relief to know that at last / the Government has set
up a committee of inquiry to / examine the conditions that exist
between our industry and the / National Health Service. One
important aspect that will have to / be considered is the value
of research. It is impossible / to put a price on the many new   50
drugs which / have helped in saving life and in reducing absence
from / work but these new drugs can only be found by / scientific
research and the cost of this work is increasing / as the standards
of safety rise higher and higher.

9

100   From / our point of view the success of our manufacturing enterprise / depends on a flow of new products for both the / home and overseas markets. We are now spending about one / million pounds a year on research and much of this / is in the

150   nature of a long-term investment since / results do not follow immediately. The cost involved in such / work must, therefore, be regarded as a necessary item in / our annual production costs.

    We ended the year on a / strong note and I am very happy to say that / the same trend is still continuing. Everything within

200   the business / is in excellent heart; we must always be looking forward, / always anticipating the many requirements of an ever-

220   changing world. /

(*Shorthand of this passage is on p.* 71)

PASSAGE B (Tape 2—White Leader)
R.S.A. 80 *words a minute, Summer,* 1966 (II)

    We are all accustomed by now to the man-made / fibres, nylon and terylene, but now we are promised another / even more remarkable. A Swedish firm has produced a fibre / from stainless steel so fine that it can be woven / into stockings, carpets and

50   even clothes. The great difference is / that the steel fibre will be very durable and first / impressions are that it is as soft to the touch / as any other material.

    The first of these steel textiles / will be produced this year and it is likely to / be used at first to make carpets, particularly

100   for hotels / and other public places where a normal carpet cannot be / expected to last very long.

    This discovery has been hailed / as comparable in significance to the first discovery of synthetic / fibres and if present anticipations are borne out the production / of textile steel could become

150   a major part of the / output of the steel industry in the more
160   advanced countries. /

(*Shorthand of this passage is on p.* 72)

PASSAGE C (Tape 2—White Leader)
R.S.A. 80 *words a minute, Summer,* 1966 (III)

    For the past four years a pair of swallows have / made their summer quarters in a wooden hut in my / garden. This is just opposite and quite close to my / bedroom window. During the

10

day the door and one window / of the hut are left open; at night
the door **/** is locked but the window is left wide open. One / wet   50
night recently I was in my bedroom when I / heard a fluttering
of wings behind the curtains which were / drawn. On account of
the rain the windows were open / only about two inches. On
inquiry I found one of **/** the baby swallows which had evidently   100
taken the wrong turning / on his way back home. When I drew
back the / curtains he flew round the room several times in a /
dazed sort of fashion, probably dazzled by the electric light. /
He then settled on the curtain rail and within a **/** minute he was   150
fast asleep. I switched on the light / about three in the morning
but this did not disturb / him in the slightest. I was fully awake
before seven / but he did not stir until an hour later when / the
wireless was switched on in the kitchen downstairs. He **/** seemed   200
puzzled at first but after flying round the room / once or twice
he found his way out by the / window. Shortly afterwards the
whole family of swallows assembled on / the gutter just above
the window and it seemed clear / that my young visitor was tell-
ing his parents where he **/** had spent the night. It seemed almost   250
a human drama. /   260

(*Shorthand of this passage is on p.* 72)

PASSAGE D (Tape 2—White Leader)

R.S.A. 80 *words a minute, Autumn,* 1966 (I)   90 ,

It is always pleasing to report an increase in profits / even
though I had hoped that the improvement would have / been
greater. In common with most manufacturing firms we have /
suffered gravely from a shortage of labour and this has / greatly
limited our expansion. The position has been made worse **/** by the   50
difficulty in obtaining supplies in sufficient quantities and / on
time. This is a serious restriction on the efficient / use of such
labour as is available for nothing is / more expensive than highly
paid labour standing idle waiting for / raw materials.

We have come to the conclusion that it **/** will be necessary to   100
transfer certain plant to areas where / there is more likelihood
of recruiting additional labour. This will / not mean cheaper production but it is necessary in order / to satisfy the demands of our
customers, and to utilize / machinery which is at present standing
idle. This appears to **/** be the only way we can continue to ex-   150
pand and / to take advantage of the opportunities presented to us.

11

During / the past year the demand for most of our products / has been good, and although there were some signs of / a decline
200 in this demand I take the view that, **/** over the coming years, there will be a continuing increase / in the requirements for the type of goods we supply. /

This year, we do not have to provide for income / tax on dividends as provision was made in previous years. / We therefore
250 have only to reserve for corporation tax and **/** this we have done at the maximum rate anticipated.

Your / directors are recommending an increased final dividend, bringing the total / up to fifteen per cent, which we hope to
280 maintain. /

(*Shorthand of this passage is on p.* 73)

PASSAGE E (Tape 2—White Leader)

R.S.A. 80 *words a minute, Autumn,* 1966 (II)

(2°

The story of carpet manufacturing in Great Britain over the / last few years is one of steady expansion, until in / 1965 there was a sudden upsurge of production / and sales. With housing still on the priority list it / is likely that carpet sales will soon amount
50 to one **/** hundred and fifty million square yards annually. One reason for / the anticipated growth is the vast increase in production of / tufted carpets. Produced on what are, in effect, giant sewing / machines working at an amazing rate, this type costs
100 considerably / less to make but the relatively low price is not **/** the main appeal. Through research and experiment in manufacturing techniques / they have become carpets in their own right. After the / early days of plain colours only, the dawn of pattern / began to emerge with the discovery of a new process / which
150 has recently been perfected, and these new-style carpets **/** com-
160 pete with Axminsters and Wiltons on their own ground. /

(*Shorthand of this passage is on p.* 74)

PASSAGE F (Tape 2—White Leader)

R.S.A. 80 *words a minute, Autumn,* 1966 (III)

We in Great Britain like to think that we live / in a democratic country. We live in a society, we / believe, in which the views of ordinary people count for / something, have some influence on those who are responsible for / local government. It is true that

12

very few councils are / likely to embark on a course of action   50
which promises / to be widely unpopular or to offend too many
people, / who, in the last resort, have the final word through /
the ballot box. But how much notice do they take / regarding the
scores of every-day decisions? A wide-awake / press can be very   100
helpful: it hears about things in / advance, it publicizes them, it
awakens and alerts the local / inhabitants. But it does not attend
committee meetings where most / decisions are really taken. It
does get copies of the / minutes but these are not always very
informative.

Local Government / will never be perfect but let those respon-   150
sible for it / remember that decisions affect people, and let people
remember they / must go to the polls, and that their responsibility
does / not end there. Local Government will then be on the / way
to becoming as democratic as we think it is. /   200

(Shorthand of this passage is on p. 75)

PASSAGE G (Tape 2—White Leader)

R.S.A. 80 *words a minute, Easter,* 1967 (I)

May I try to give you a bird's eye view / of all that is involved
in managing this vast enterprise / of ours? Size itself brings problems for we have to / deal with large numbers of men and women
who have / to work in harmony when mastering difficult techniques in the / many different sections. In all this we must make   50
sure / that we gain, not lose, from the size and complex / nature
of our business.

Our managers must be capable of / looking into the future,
sometimes into the very distant future, / with a mixture of im-
agination and common sense. At the / same time they must not   100
lose sight of the problems / of today. This is a business in which
small changes / can have effects quite out of proportion to the
size / of those changes. It is a business in which "million" / and even
"billion" are words in everyday use to measure / both the quan-   150
tities and the expenditure in which we are / accustomed to deal.
Our managers continue to need the same / qualities which were
most needed in the past but now / the problems are more complex
and the questions more searching. / As I have said we have always
had to be / far-sighted but in the past it was an art, / in that we   200
were often guided by a "hunch" or / inspiration. Today it is much
closer to a science and / we put great effort into reducing guess-
work and to / improving the chances that our decisions will be the

13

250 right **/** ones, for very often we are risking millions of pounds /
in a particular project.

Our principal aim is to make / a profit. This calls for a firm
but delicate touch / on the wheel, a sober view of the present,
300 a / bold view of the future and a right judgement of **/** the factors
which bear upon the business twenty-four hours / a day. For
example, more than ever before we have / to be sensitive to the
changes in political outlook as / well as the aspirations of peoples
340 all over the world. /

(*Shorthand of this passage is on p.* 76)

PASSAGE H (Tape 2—White Leader)

R.S.A. 80 *words a minute, Easter,* 1967 (II)

There are many causes of accidents on the roads but / it has
been stated on good authority that faulty tyres / are responsible
for about one-third of all accidents involving / motor vehicles.
Despite this, the amount of care and consideration / the average
50 owner gives to them is often of a **/** very casual nature. How often
does one see a car / parked in such a way that the sharp edge of /
the kerb is forced into the side-wall of the / tyre. Even though
the tread may still have more than / a sufficient depth of rubber
100 on it the casing may **/** have been damaged and may give way
under the stress / of fast driving. A burst tyre, when a car is /
going at a high speed, can be very serious indeed, / not only for
the passengers but for innocent people on / the road, for the car
150 may suddenly dive towards the **/** near-side ditch, or there may be
a collision with / a car or a lorry coming in the opposite direc-
tion. /

It is essential, too, that every motorist should concentrate
during / the whole of the time he is at the wheel. / Too often one
200 sees the careless way so many motorists **/** have of laying a couple
of fingers on the steering / wheel and resting the elbow on the
window ledge. They / are trying to show what old hands they are
at / this motoring game. But should an emergency occur the car /
250 is in the ditch before they can regain control. Driving **/** on the con-
gested roads of today is something that necessitates / the fullest
concentration at all times. One idle moment at / the wheel has
often been the cause of a frightful / crash involving not only loss
but also injury to pedestrians / who just happen to be there at
300 that very moment. **/**

(*Shorthand of this passage is on p.* 77)

14

PASSAGE A (Tape 2—Red Leader)

R.S.A. 80 *words a minute, Summer,* 1967 (I)

Our last business year covered a period of fifty-three / weeks
and at first we were hard put to it / to keep pace with the demand for glass. The development / of new and cheaper plastics
has provided manufacturers with an / excellent opportunity to
enter fresh markets and in some cases / these must be at the ex-   50
pense of glass, and I / have no doubt you will expect me to comment on / the relative roles of glass and plastic containers.

Increased competition / in the High Street is speeding the
trend towards self-/service stores where, it is said, more than fifty
per / cent of purchases are made on impulse. As a result, / an   100
attractive container is becoming more and more important as /
it clearly provides a powerful stimulus to sales. It must / give
complete protection to the product, have mass consumer appeal, /
and the price must be right. These three conditions are, / I am   150
sure, fulfilled by the glass container.

Developments are / in progress at our works, including the
erection of a / workshop for the manufacture of plastics, and we
shall shortly / be well equipped to supply the manufacturer with
whatever type / of container, in plastic or glass, suits his particular
product. /   200

(*Shorthand of this passage is on p.* 78)

PASSAGE B (Tape 2—Red Leader)

R.S.A. 80 *words a minute, Summer,* 1967 (II)

3.11.82
class reading + speeds

We had not had such a glorious day for five / summers. The
temperature was eighty in the shade, quite unusual / for this
mountain top. I had been out looking at / the horses and having   90.
checked them over I walked up / to our north-east corner where
a little stream forms / the boundary of our farm. I sat down at   50
a / point where the stream opens out into a pool which / the
horses occasionally use for drinking. In the pool I / counted
several trout playing about quite happily.

Presently a large / mink appeared on the opposite side of the
stream and / the trout vanished in an instant. That was the first /   100
time I had seen a mink in these parts although / we had heard
that several had escaped from a mink / farm many miles away to
the south.

15

This was indeed / bad luck for the trout, for mink are to
150   trout / what foxes are to chickens. When a fox gets into / a hen-
roost he cannot eat more than one at / a time and he cannot carry
more than one away. / That does not hinder him from slaying all
200   the occupants. / So it is with mink. He can satisfy himself on /
one medium-sized trout but he continues until he has / destroyed
220   as many as will satisfy his lust for killing. /

(*Shorthand of this passage is on p.* 79)

PASSAGE C (Tape 2—Red Leader)

R.S.A. 80 *words a minute, Summer,* 1967 (III)

I suppose all of us, as customers of oil companies, / are rather
inclined to think of them as rolling in / wealth but when we are
taking this view we are / sometimes a little apt to forget that this
50   wealth does / not descend of its own accord from the heavens or /
even well up from the earth, or, for that matter, / from the base
of the sea, but that it results / from the extremely hard work of
a very large number / of people.
    If I may presume to say so, we / have achieved a very con-
100   siderable success and it cannot be / stressed too often that it is
on such commercial enterprises / as ours that the prosperity of
this country does, in / a large measure, depend. Our contribution
this year to the / balance of payments amounts to eighty million
pounds.
    I think / this is a matter for congratulation to the management,
150   and / for gratitude on the part of the community. As for / gratitude what is it but a lively sense of future / favours? From what
we have learned today I do not / think that even that form of
gratitude is misplaced and / I have no doubt in my own mind
200   that we / are greatly indebted both to the management and to
220   all / engaged in this great task for a magnificent year's work. /

(*Shorthand of this passage is on p.* 80)

PASSAGE D (Tape 2—Red Leader)

R.S.A. 80 *words a minute, Autumn,* 1967 (I)

Our total turnover increased by more than twelve per cent, /
to which increase both sides of our business contributed. The /
rate of growth in the frozen food side of our / business continued

16

and for the first time since we began / operations in this field, the production of frozen foods earned **/** more than half of the trading profits for the year. /   50

Although many countries, in the interests of their own people,/ introduced import licences which affected us severely, our export sales, / though small in relation to our total turnover, showed an / increase of nearly twenty per cent, which, in all the **/** circum-   100 stances, can be called progress.

The relationship with our growers / continues to be good. This is soundly based upon an / understanding of each other's point of view, but, at the / same time, on a realization that both growers and the / company share the same task of disposing of our prod- ucts **/** in a steady flow. We have an extensive range of / products,   150 because time-saving foods, coupled with variety, are what / the modern housewife demands and can pay for today. I / am doing my best to give her what she wants / at a fair price consistent with sound quality.

It might **/** have been thought that increased consumption of   200 quick frozen foods / would have reduced the sale of canned foods but several / of our most important traditional lines of canned vegetables show / an encouraging trend. If world conditions were more stable I / would say, without hedging, that the outlook was most encouraging **/** and that much higher profits could be ex-   250 pected with confidence. /   260

(*Shorthand of this passage is on p. 81*)

10/11/82

PASSAGE E (Tape 2—Red Leader)

R.S.A. 80 *words a minute, Autumn,* 1967 (II)

It is no wonder that many British exporters are under / heavy fire for poor selling efforts when they continue to / support the very old belief that there is no need / to use any language but English in their sales literature. / Some time ago one of my clients was expecting a **/** group of some half-dozen men from South   50 America, all / of whom spoke English very well. He asked me, urgently, / to add a commentary in Spanish to a film he / wished to show his visitors. He also invited me to / be present, thinking I might be interested. I was.

Arriving **/** at the office I was introduced to the group who /   100 did indeed speak excellent English, and in his little theatre / the film began. When the commentator started speaking in Spanish / the reaction of the visitors was audible. At the end / of the show

17

150 they could hardly say enough about the **/** great courtesy of my
client in taking such trouble to / show them a film in their own
language. I believe / a most satisfactory contract resulted.

There seems little doubt that / remarks to the effect that it is
unnecessary to sell / to a man in his own language, whether in
200 literature **/** or in films, are but very feeble excuses for inaction. /
220 There is every need for this rewarding form of courtesy. /

(*Shorthand of this passage is on p.* 82)

PASSAGE F (Tape 2—Red Leader)

R.S.A. 80 *words a minute, Autumn,* 1967 (III)

I was interested to read the other day that the / attitude in
Britain to the working women was Victorian, or / even worse. I
should like to mention that, in the / part of the world I know
well, India, the attitude / to the working woman is far from
50 Victorian. Since the **/** independence of India, women, in business,
the professions and politics, / have been given full equality with
men.

As a European / woman running a manufacturing business I
have found no discrimination / against women. Not only do they
enjoy equal opportunity but / they are also given the respect that
100 Indian men have **/** always given their women-folk.

In one field, taxation, they / are far better treated. The earned
income of a wife / is taxed entirely separately and it is high time
that / women in Britain insisted on reform in this department.
British / women should also realize that some of their Indian
150 sisters **/** have surpassed them in obtaining equality, both economi-
160 cally and socially. /

(*Shorthand of this passage is on p.* 83)

PASSAGE G (Tape 2—Red Leader)

R.S.A. 80 *words a minute, Easter,* 1968 (I)

I am very glad to tell you that our new / reservoir, about which
you have been receiving progress reports for / the past six years,
50 is now in full use. This / is, in effect, a large lake with a surface
area / of over one thousand acres; it adds greatly to the **/** attraction of the district and has already become the place / to visit at

18

holidays and week-ends. We have carried / out much landscape gardening and the quiet beauty of the / place is much appreciated by visitors.

As one might expect, / all this has created traffic problems on the roads leading / to the reservoir. The local councils are now 100 busy considering / plans to cope, and it may be necessary for us / to provide additional car parks. We are also giving serious / thought to the provision of footpaths and possibly picnic areas / where we would be better able to control the litter / problem. 150

It has been decided to permit fishing, and last / year the reservoir was stocked with trout and further stocking / will be carried out shortly. At our last meeting we / decided that sailing on the new lake would be an / added attraction and a working party was set up. Already / the large amount of information 200 collected indicates that there is / a considerable number of sailors in the district and this / summer small boats with white sails will become a pleasant / feature.

We will provide a stand for boats on the / north shore as well as other facilities, which we will / lease to a sailing club which is 250 being formed. It / will also be necessary for us to provide a road / to give access to the north shore.

In all these / matters we are being guided by the principle that the / reservoir should be used to the utmost by members of / the 300 public, provided that nothing is done to impede the / company in carrying out its duty to provide, for the / inhabitants of our large district, water which is pure and / wholesome.

We have official sanction for all we are doing. / 340

(*Shorthand of this passage is on p. 83*)

PASSAGE H (Tape 2—Red Leader)

R.S.A. 80 *words a minute, Easter,* 1968 (II)

For some years the chemical industry has been growing rapidly / and there is every reason to believe that this growth / will continue, but it will be necessary for us to / invest a very large amount of capital. Such investment has / always been necessary with normal growth but recently there has / been a quite unusual advance in 50 methods of manufacture. This / means that we have to replace plant which, in the / normal course of events, might have been expected to give / service for some years more. The new plants can be / operated at much lower cost but, in providing these improved / plants, the resources of the industry, in terms of both / 100 finance and staff, are very greatly strained.

19

We are faced / with the necessity of offsetting the increase
in wages and / other costs while at the same time we have to /
150 meet intensive competition. We can only do this by adopting /
newer and cheaper processes as these are discovered.

It would / be surprising if, in a period of such rapid change, /
our judgements were always right and if we suffered no / setbacks
or delays. The present phase is common to chemical / firms
200 throughout the world but, with our increasing knowledge of /
these large-scale plants, we hope to pass through this / phase with
success in the reasonably near future.

We think / it prudent policy to provide the necessary funds from
our / own resources. Fortunately we have built up over the years /
250 large amounts in depreciation and in future we shall be / compelled to rely mainly on this method to provide new / capital
expenditure. Having reduced our costs in the light of / current
conditions, we do not believe that we will have / to ask the shareholders for further finance for some time / but we are sure a
300 brighter picture will emerge soon. /

(*Shorthand of this passage is on p.* 84)

PASSAGE A (Tape 3—White Leader)

R.S.A. 80 *words a minute, Whitsun,* 1968 (I)

The past year has been an eventful one. Owing to / the shortage
of female labour in the London area and / the huge increase in
local rates we have had to / dispose of the factory there but the
staff displaced have / not been forgotten.
50 The duty on imported paper has now / been eliminated and
for the first time for more than / thirty years the industry has to
face foreign competition without / the shelter of tariffs. There
were two choices open to / us: we could fade out quietly from
the scene or / we could develop and concentrate on those sectors
100 of the / paper trade in which foreigners do not have the great /
advantage of producing their own raw materials.

We have chosen / the latter alternative and as we must have the
correct / tools to do the job we are committed to heavy / expen-
150 diture on paper-making machinery, the benefit of which we / shall
not reap for some time. We are engaged in / an expanding market
and I have not the slightest doubt / that your company can look
180 forward to a glowing future. /

(*Shorthand of this passage is on p.* 86)

20

PASSAGE B (Tape 3—White Leader)

R.S.A. 80 words a minute, Whitsun, 1968 (II)

In my first year at university I teamed up with / a girl from
Canada and she invited me to spend / the long vacation at her
home. It was a new / experience for me to cross the Atlantic by
jet and / it created a feeling of confusion because of the necessary /   50
alteration of clocks and the serving of what seemed to / me continuous meals.

Adjustment to the change was gradual. The / first two weeks
were like any holiday abroad: new experiences / all the time and
special treatment for me as a / visitor. Then I began to adjust
myself to the new / way of life. My first shock was that the fact /   100
that we speak English on both sides of the Atlantic / is very often
misleading. I became self-conscious about my / accent and was
sometimes asked to repeat words just for / amusement, and
occasionally I failed to make myself understood.

Everything / seemed to be on a larger scale. To buy a / quarter   150
of sweets is virtually unheard of; flour would be / ordered by the
sack and similarly with nearly every commodity. / Despite such
differences I came to feel so much at / home and such a member
of the family that leaving / was a real wrench. I had come to share   200
things / with them though I was still rather proudly introduced
as / their visitor from the old country. I had even been / allotted
a particular family task as chief berry picker, strawberries / first
and later raspberries.

As an ordinary tourist I would / doubtless have seen the usual   250
attractions but now I feel / I know something of the real life in
North America / and I have made lifelong friends in the New
World. /   280

(*Shorthand of this passage is on p.* 86)

PASSAGE C (Tape 3—White Leader)

R.S.A. 80 words a minute, Whitsun, 1968 (III)

Although there has been some improvement our sales are still /
running below what we deem to be normal but that / does not
apply to our instant coffee which, in a / highly competitive market,
is continuing to find increasing favour. I / should remind you,
however, that our instant coffee sales are / a relatively small pro-   50
portion of our turnover.

New processing machinery / has been installed and further changes are now being carried / out. Much attention is being given to the packaging of / our products and a new range has been introduced to / meet more precisely the needs of certain of our
100 customers. /

The profitability of our business is affected both by volume / of sales and the price of our raw ingredients, particularly / coffee. The workings of the international coffee agreement have succeeded / in stabilizing prices but present indications are that coffee will / cost us more in the current year.
150 There are also / other factors at work and we continue to seek new / methods and to develop new products which could help to / compensate for any lower profit margins from our traditional
180 lines. /

(Shorthand of this passage is on p. 87)

PASSAGE D (Tape 3—White Leader)

R.S.A. 80 words a minute, Summer, 1968 (I)

We could not exist without tourists, and therefore we should / be used to the annual pattern by now, but we / always seem to be taken by surprise by the crowds / which flood suddenly into our peaceful little town. They are / so numerous that we natives feel
50 almost submerged and we / have learned to complete all our shopping before the visitors / emerge from hotels, boarding houses and caravans.

During the morning / the crowds are increased as the daily coaches arrive, while / people with their own transport spill out from the car / parks, spread over the large village green and along
100 the / promenade. The motor launches, brimming over with holiday-makers, put / out on the lake. Everywhere there is noise and bustle / for everyone is determined to have a lovely time, whether / it rains or shines.

The daily trippers are never still / for they have to cram every
150 experience into a few / short hours. The homeward journey starts about six o'clock and / towards the end of the season the whole place seems / suddenly to empty about tea-time.

At week-ends there / are still some cars parked round the edge
200 of the / lake but these also soon stop coming. The village again / assumes the air of an animal about to take its / winter sleep as
220 a refuge from the cold and rain. /

(Shorthand of this passage is on p. 88)

22

PASSAGE E (Tape 3—White Leader)

R.S.A. 80 *words a minute, Summer,* 1968 (II)

I was in America last summer and again this spring / and I
found that many business leaders seemed surprised to / learn that
Britain's trade balance was still adverse. Most Americans / do not
realize that the problem of our balance of / payments, like their
own, is so largely due to expenditure / on defence and the aid   50
given to underdeveloped countries. They / are quite unaware of
the fact that a gap on / actual trade has been a regular feature
of the picture / for nearly two hundred years. Almost every year
this is / more than balanced by the value of the banking and /   100
insurance services we render to the rest of the world. /

In recent years we seem to have taken a delight / in emphasiz-
ing each month's trade balance without drawing attention to /
the value of these earnings in the national housekeeping. People /
abroad take the figures at their face value and, as / a consequence 150
of their ignorance, look upon Britain as a / country always in
trouble. It is high time that our / position was presented abroad
in a much more accurate light. /   180

(*Shorthand of this passage is on p.* 89)

PASSAGE F (Tape 3—White Leader)

R.S.A. 80 *words a minute, Autumn,* 1968 (II)

It was, I must now confess, a pure accident when, / with a flick
of his elbow, my young son sent / the little plate spinning to the
floor. As I swept / up the pieces I sadly reflected that this was
the / last item of a tea-set given to us as / a wedding-present   50
sixteen years before. I loved it so / much that I could remember
the circumstances in which each / of the thirty-eight pieces had
been broken. It was / but short-lived when compared with my
grandmother's tea-set, / bought seventy years ago, which now
adorns my china cabinet. / Of course, hers only appears on the   100
very best occasions / and in well-behaved company. I remembered
with a curious / satisfaction that I never broke a piece.

Whenever a favourite / treasure is shattered I moon about the
house, sometimes for / days on end. Yet I think these lovely
things ought / to be used. Surely the children should be allowed   150
to / see and feel and clasp their hands around cups that / are well
designed and artistically coloured. How, otherwise, can they /
learn the pleasure to be derived from fine china, one / of the most
civilized of the arts?

23

200   I am now **/** busy collecting a new tea-set. I am searching for /
old cups in a particular pink lustre, with designs of / trees and
cottages and windmills. They are hard to come / by nowadays
but the final result will be a bright / landscape in lustre on our
250   tea-table. Slowly I am **/** beginning to learn the origin of the china
I possess / but an even more absorbing task is to find out / what
280   great house had owned and used it before me. /

(*Shorthand of this passage is on p.* 90)

PASSAGE G (Tape 3—White Leader)

R.S.A. 80 *words a minute, Whitsun,* 1969 (I)

     I have one of those watches that never need winding. / It has
been my trusty servant for years, and what / is more, it is plain
proof of something which I / firmly believe in — that life is full of
50   magic. My / watch has just gone on and on but I have **/** never
tried to discover or to understand how it works / but, instead,
have been well content to believe that it / is a miracle, not capable
of being explained but just / a wonderful and magical thing.
     Suddenly, one morning, I had / quite a shock to find it had
100   stopped but after **/** a moment's thought I decided that it required
cleaning. At / the earliest opportunity, therefore, I called at the
establishment where / it had been bought and asked if it could
be / put right. I was assured that my watch was in / good order
150   but that it was out of oil. Two **/** hours later I boarded a train and
got into conversation / with a fellow-traveller who had just returned from the / United States. He told me he had met many
interesting / people and one of the most unusual was a man / in
200   the oil business. This did not arouse much interest **/** in me until
he went on to say that his / acquaintance was not engaged in the
ordinary oil business but / made the most expensive oil, the kind
used in watches / that do not need winding. How extraordinary!
This was one / of those strange events with which life sometimes
250   faces us. **/** For want of a better expression I call them moments /
of truth. At such times we may pause to think / of the many
services and amenities unknown a generation ago, / but it is only
for a moment and we will / continue to take for granted what-
300   ever miracles are offered us. **/**

(*Shorthand of this passage is on p.* 91)

PASSAGE H (Tape 3—White Leader)

R.S.A. 80 *words a minute, Whitsun,* 1969 (II)

It can be argued that any organization providing goods for /
an expanding market would have to be very inefficient indeed /
to fail to achieve some small level of profit. The / air transport
industry has been in an expanding market for / a long time but
there is one important factor governing / airline operations that   50
does not apply to ordinary commercial undertakings. / An airline exists to provide one thing only — an airline / seat on a particular plane, that is, a flight from / one place to another. Immediately that particular flight leaves the / ground at its starting point,
any empty seat represents a / direct loss of revenue; the airline   100
cannot put that seat / back on the shelf in the hope that another
customer / will come forward and buy it another day; its useful-
ness / as a source of income has disappeared.

This particular factor / is common to all transport undertakings.
The proportion of seats / filled to those offered for sale is known   150
as the / "load factor", and it is especially vital to airline travel. /
A fall of only one per cent in the load / factor over the year can
often mean the loss of / one million pounds or more in revenue
to a company. / Time-tables have to be made out some time in /   200
advance and may run for three or six months. A / change in conditions, such as a reduction in the foreign / travel allowance, or a
decline in the economic conditions of / a country may reduce
considerably the number of people travelling. / In such circum-   250
stances the airline can make no significant economies; / the
flight personnel cannot be reduced in number and all / other costs
remain the same. A small fall in the / load factor from 60·2 per
cent to 5/9·3 per cent was sufficient to bring about / a loss on a   300
year's working of one of the / largest British airlines. An increase
in the load factor could / result in much higher profits or, what
the travelling public / would doubtless prefer, a very substantial
reduction in air fares. /   340

(*Shorthand of this passage is on p.* 92)

PASSAGE A (Tape 3—Red Leader)

R.S.A. **80** *words a minute, Summer,* 1969 (I)

A survey a few years ago suggested that sixty-three / per cent
of people buying a car for the first / time buy second-hand, the
greatest market being the eighteen / to thirty age group. The

surprising thing is that, whereas / with house purchase every pre-
50   caution is taken to buy wisely, **/** when it comes to buying a car
caution is thrown / to the wind, the goods being valued solely on
their / looks, a salesman's word and a short run round the / block.
In some cases all is well, but far too / often eagerness gets the
better of common sense.
100   The faults **/** to look for are rust and body deterioration. Between them / they can be costly to cure and it is doubtful / if
rust can be entirely halted. There are areas liable / to rust which
can be seen by the average person, / the bottom of doors, under
150   carpets and sometimes along the **/** tops of front wings.
Of course, no buyer of a / used car can expect it to be in a
brand-/new condition and he should expect to pay for work /
which represents fair wear and tear and which is necessary / as the
200   result of apparent use. One should never rely **/** on the speedometer
reading for it often has to be / changed, and this means that the
mileage at the date / of change is not shown on the new instru-
240   ment. All / in all, the only safe course is to get advice. /

(*Shorthand of this passage is on p.* 93)

PASSAGE B (Tape 3—Red Leader)

R.S.A. 80 *words a minute, Summer,* 1969 (II)

During the last months of the year it became necessary / to
reduce the production of clay bricks but once demand / revived
in the spring it became difficult to increase output / quickly
enough to meet the sudden increase in demand. One / particular
50   order for the first phase of a major development **/** project was so
large that it was decided, as a / temporary measure, to set up our
own manufacturing plant on / the site.
The demand for drain pipes for land drainage / remained high
and deliveries during the year reached record levels. / Some two-
100   thirds of the total pipe drainage schemes now **/** make use of our
products but because of their quality / and low price further
room still exists for expansion.
Once / again our Research and Technical Department has played
an important / part both in improving the quality and efficiency
of our / existing products and in investigating new building mater-
150   ials. It is **/** little use making good bricks at a low cost if / they
are not employed efficiently and more and more of / our research

26

is being directed to this end. Many and / varied problems arise
and our Research Department is continually providing / technical
assistance to builders, to architects and to civil engineers. /   200

(Shorthand of this passage is on p. 94)

PASSAGE C (Tape 3—Red Leader)

R.S.A. 80 *words a minute, Summer,* 1969 (III)

Dear Tom,
   I understand from the general office that you / will be staying
in Newcastle for another three nights before / returning home, so
I thought you might like to consider / the enclosed letter carefully,
and then take action on it / as soon as you can. I suppose I could
have / left a message at the hotel for you to telephone / me but,   50
as you will see when you read the / letter, it is one of those matters that really requires / some first-hand thought and action.
   It is just one / more sad tale in the history of our recently
dismissed / sales representative in the area. I have just been look-   100
ing / through it all again. On the evidence we now have, / it seems
that he cashed cheques with customers, but the / cheques were
later dishonoured. He also entered into private arrangements / with
one or two customers to share discount that was / not payable,   150
increased his expenses by making dishonest deals with / garages
to record petrol sales that were never made, and / on at least three
occasions was extremely rude to customers. /
   I leave you to get over there at once and / do your very best to
straighten things out.
                                    Yours sincerely, /   200

(Shorthand of this passage is on p. 95)

PASSAGE D (Tape 3—Red Leader)

R.S.A. 80 *words a minute, Autumn,* 1969 (I)

   Last year we were without rain for a very long / time. Indeed,
it was the worst drought in our history. / As a result our main
export crops had a very / bad year. To make matters worse, the
market for these / products has become more competitive while
we have not yet / been successful in reducing costs of production   50
in Jamaica.

One / has only to look round our city to observe the / tendency towards tall buildings with many storeys and probably you / will agree with me that these modern, well-designed buildings / have
100 done much to beautify our island, and the architects / responsible deserve great credit. Their achievements give us a feeling / of immense satisfaction in knowing that much of the freedom / they enjoy in design is due to the variety of / materials available, not the least of which is our own / main product, cement.
150 Our country continues to attract money from / overseas investors and it is beyond question that our company's / great success has made a significant contribution to the image / of our island as a good and profitable area for / investment. Over twenty new enterprises were started last year and / some of these are
200 very large indeed. Our economic growth / to date is the result of the efforts of our / people who strive always to be successful in their undertakings / and are not satisfied with anything short of the best. / We must aim high for if we do so we / shall certainly
250 achieve more than if we just muddle on / aimlessly, hoping for the best. The people of our island / have courage and ability and, above all, respect for the / human rights of others. These good qualities, combined with hard / work and sound leadership, will, in the coming years, all / help to build up a very healthy economy
300 in Jamaica. /

(*Shorthand of this passage is on p.* 96)

PASSAGE E (Tape 3—Red Leader)

R.S.A. 80 *words a minute, Autumn,* 1969 (II)

It seems that man's oldest means of transport, the horse, / may come into his own again. The increase in running / costs of motor vehicles has forced firms to look at / the question of alternatives. One firm of brewers has five / pairs of horses which annually de-
50 liver ten thousand tons of / beer within a three-mile radius. Management consultants called in / to review the whole organization were expected to recommend that / the horses be dispensed with but they found that, within / their limits, the horses were more economic.
A fundamental factor / in the situation is depreciation. A suit-
100 able commercial vehicle costs / about fifteen hundred pounds, and after seven years a replacement / is necessary. A pair of heavy cart horses can be / bought for less than four hundred pounds, no road fund / licence is payable and the cost of upkeep is cheaper. /

28

The horse societies have been fighting a losing battle for / years   150
in trying to maintain the particular breed, but the / plans they
now have in hand could turn the transport / wheel full circle, at
least in the crowded city streets. /   180

(Shorthand of this passage is on p. 97)

PASSAGE F (Tape 3—Red Leader)

R.S.A. 80 words a minute, Autumn, 1969 (III)

Dear Sir,

I am pleased to be able to send / you earlier than we had promised our new catalogues of / goods for sale for the next two years.
As you / will see we have made an extensive use of colour / in
preparing these new catalogues and the mass of information /   50
that they contain has been set out in a much / more interesting
way which is also very easy to read. /

The direct mail order business continues to go on from /
success to success and it now represents more than twenty / per
cent of the whole retail market.

We are sure / that with the best use of these catalogues you   100
will / be able to increase still further the excellent results you /
achieved last year as our agent. As a further inducement / we are
increasing our commission on all annual sales over / one thousand
pounds by two per cent. Please call on / our local representative 150
for any help you need.

                                        Yours truly, /   160

(Shorthand of this passage is on p. 97)

PASSAGE G (Tape 3—Red Leader)

Additional Material, 320 *words,* 80 *words a minute*

For the last three years we have been able to / report an increase in profits but I regret that we / cannot do so on this occasion because, as you will / have seen from the accounts, the
trading profit is down / by a little over three million, five hundred
thousand pounds. / When, however, comparing the profit and   50
the output figures with / the preceding year it must be remembered
that the latter / covered fifty-three weeks, whereas the year under
review covers / only fifty-two weeks. Some reduction in profit

29

100   was not / unexpected, as we realized that we were faced with the /
       inevitable expense and difficulties of running in the new plant /
       at Manchester.
           The decline in the profit at our main / factory was brought
       about by a number of adverse factors. / Competition was very keen
       and we were fully aware that / only the highest quality and service
150   would enable us to / obtain orders. For a period we ran into
       certain manufacturing / difficulties. These problems were over-
       come. As we feel sure that / in a highly competitive market
       quality and service are the / key to success we are taking steps to
       ensure that / we shall continue to meet both these requirements.
           We have / been able to keep the plant running somewhere near
200   capacity / by increasing our export business. The alternative to
       this would / have been to curtail production to some extent. It is /
       not particularly easy to arrive at an exact calculation as / to
250   whether it is better at ridiculously low prices or / to curtail pro-
       duction. The latter is not a step we / would want to take without
       very serious consideration but it / is a possibility which we cannot
       entirely ignore. There seems / no prospect of an increase in export
       prices in the / immediate future for there is a world-wide excess
300   capacity / of steel. This is perhaps more particularly so in the /
320   flat rolled section of the industry than in any other. /

                 (*Shorthand of this passage is on p.* 98)

PASSAGE A (Tape 4—White Leader)

R.S.A. 100 *words a minute, Summer,* 1966 (I)

           A journey round the capital cities of the world reveals / that
       the world is getting smaller and smaller. The aeroplane / has almost
       annihilated both space and time. If you stand / in the main square
       of any capital city it is / often difficult to determine for a moment
50   just exactly where / you are. The same electric signs advertise the
       same products, / often with but the slightest change of name. But
       the / capital of Brazil is like no other place on earth. / Every
       country has its new towns; similarly every country tries / to attract
100   industry and citizens to its less favoured areas, / but Brazil's ver-
       sion of these laudable and universal aims is / on a different plane
       entirely. Less than ten years ago / there was no town, no village,
       not so much as / a hut on the high plateau where it now stands. /
150   The nearest human life was nearly one hundred miles away; /
       no road led to or from it; it was nothing / but a hump in the
       middle of a jungle. Now / it is a city of three hundred thousand

                                    30

people and / the country's capital. The self-contained residential areas are vivid / with activity; the commercial, industrial, and political sections have their / own distinctive character, and the   200
whole thing seems to move / as if it had a pulse beating through it. Although / it was conceived as the monument to one man it / is now the realization of all the dreams of all / the architects who ever lived.

To the inhabitants of other / capital cities such a place is still   250
a dream, for / each year as traffic grows the city gets less work-able, / less attractive. If you can drive there at all you / can't park; if you can park it is too far / from where you want to go. But neither can you / walk, really, for you will be intimidated by cars,   300
blown / at with poisonous fumes, out-shouted by the roar of / buses. So each year more of us come in for / only special occasions. But we miss it, the easy meeting-/place, crowded, rubbing shoulders indeed, full of variety and colour. /   350

(*Shorthand of this passage is on p.* 100)

PASSAGE B (Tape 4—White Leader)

R.S.A. 100 *words a minute, Summer,* 1966 (II)

You may be surprised to learn that last year our / companies throughout the world spent over one hundred million pounds / on packaging materials. Wrappers of some kind are necessary to / make goods portable and to protect them from dirt or / damage, but in these days there is much more to / it than that. Goods are   50
packed nowadays in such a / way as to make each packet as nearly as possible / unique, to be recognizable at a glance. This is what / we might call the marketing function of packaging. Over a / wide range of goods the pack, no less than its / contents, is an essential   100
part of the proposition that is / being put to the customer. In cosmetics, for example, emotion / plays an important part and the pack helps powerfully to / arouse it. If you sold face powder loose by weight / you would not make much appeal to the modern Miss. / When you buy tooth-paste in a tube you are / buying also a   150
convenient means of transferring it on to / the tooth-brush. The important thing, from our point of / view, is that the package or wrapper must be such / as will catch the eye of the shopper, who will / come to recognize it as something she desires and some-   200
thing / that she will almost automatically drop into her basket when / she is engaged in shopping in the supermarket. Each manu-facturer / wants his particular products to stand out in this way / and much thought and care are devoted to achieve this / purpose.   250

31

Some people seem to think that packaging belongs only / to the world of affluence. There are those who think / that once it gets beyond the essentials it becomes an / expensive trifle, something that ought not to be taken seriously / unless society has
300 more money than sense. They maintain that **/** it inflates prices without doing anything worthwhile in return / and therefore consider it a downright nuisance. We know, however, / that its cost is amply justified if it helps to / bring about the full economies of mass production and mass / distribution.
350 How heavy, in fact, is the burden laid upon **/** the consumer by the cost of packaging? The simplest wrapper / for margarine accounts for 1·7 per cent of / the price charged, while the comparable figure for one of / our main brands of tooth-paste is 5·3 /
400 per cent. This is a very small proportion when it **/** is remembered that goods, while on the shelf, must be / protected from damage in handling, as well as from the / harmful effects of light and sometimes heat. Another important factor / in effective packaging is to ensure that, even in unfavourable / conditions, the product
450 retains its freshly-packed flavour and aroma. **/**

(*Shorthand of this passage is on p.* 101)

PASSAGE C (Tape 4—White Leader)

R.S.A. 100 *words a minute, Autumn,* 1966 (I)

The average British farmer of today, whose family connections with / farming extend, perhaps, through many generations is naturally anxious to / settle any son of his, who has inherited the traditions / of the land, upon a farm of his own. This /
50 has been the pattern of country life for centuries. From **/** the human angle it seems natural and logical, for, if / anyone has a right to the land, it is the / man whose traditions and outlook come of it. The possibility / of such a man acquiring the land for this purpose / becomes more and more remote.
100 The same difficulties arise with **/** tenant farmers, some of whom have been tenants on estates, / going back for many generations. It has been, hitherto, the / natural way of things that, as a man came to / retirement, his son took over the tenancy, but this
150 once / well-established feature is coming to an end. Now he **/** is warned that, on his retirement, the farm will revert / to the estate, and it is by no means uncommon / for ruthless pressures to be put upon him to retire / prematurely. Farming families who have been

associated with a particular / estate, sometimes for centuries, disappear from the scene and the / farm is incorporated into a new and vaster enterprise. 200

Many / people would like to see farming organized into producing units / of enormous size but farmers are beginning to forge their / own weapons to defend their stake in the land. I / have faith to believe that, while health and enjoyment in / what they are doing remain, they will not easily be / pushed out. If they are, our villages will become dormitories / for those working in the large cities, and the farm / worker will then become a mere factory hand. 250

Outside my / room as I write I hear the thrush announcing the / coming of spring; I look across the fields green with / winter corn; I see men pushing ahead with the last / of the spring ploughing and sowing; the trees stand dreaming / on the hills; I can just see the sloping roof-/tops of the farm-house which shelters a lifelong friend / of mine. There is no sign in this peaceful scene / of the immense struggle that is going on in British / farming at the present time. 300 350 375

(*Shorthand of this passage is on p.* 102)

PASSAGE D (Tape 4—White Leader)

R.S.A. 100 *words a minute, Autumn,* 1966 (II)

If we make a forecast today of the trends and / development of an industry we have the advantage that no / one can say we are wrong until long after our / forecast is forgotten. It is doubtful, indeed, whether anybody writing / ten or fifteen years ago could have given anything like / accurate forecasts of the dramatic changes which have overtaken the / textile industry in the past two or three years. The / task is doubly difficult because the industry is in a / state of flux. It has been undergoing a basic change / from being an industry employing large numbers of workers to / one in which the emphasis is on machinery and partial / automation. Not only so, the control of the industry is / now mainly in the hands of the producers of man-/made fibres. Before their advent, the return on capital was / seldom sufficient to allow for a proper renewal of plant / and machinery while labour was used in such large numbers. / This was especially so after the cotton industry moved from / a position without serious competition to one where it had / to fight price-cutting from many low-cost countries. 50 100 150

Recent / estimates that have been made of the probable growth
200 of / the industry suggest a figure of forty per cent over / the next
fifteen years. The land available for the production / of the natural
fibres, wool, cotton, flax and jute, is / limited. On this analysis,
therefore, we can look forward to / a considerable increase in the
250 production of the synthetic fibres. /

(Shorthand of this passage is on p. 103)

PASSAGE E (Tape 4—White Leader)

R.S.A. 100 *words a minute, Autumn,* 1966 (III)

We have been appointed by the government to act as / an independent body to advise Industry on how best to / use our
energy resources. The simplest form of energy is / human muscle
power and it is a function of management / to replace this, so that
50 the increase in productivity, so / greatly desired, can be gained by
fewer rather than more / people.
The first sign that there may be natural gas / and oil under the
North Sea has led to the / term "bonanza" being used, an exciting
word but one which / I deprecate in this context. "Bonanza"
100 suggests plenty to waste. / Even if our island were found to be
surrounded by / gas and oil, as well as largely being made of / coal,
the new source of energy would be required to / be used with
care. Plenty is no excuse for prodigality. / Unless something un-
150 foreseen occurs it is a long time to / the end of the world and a
lot of fuel / will be needed to develop our industrial potential
175 even over / the remainder of this century.

(Shorthand of this passage is on p. 104)

PASSAGE F (Tape 4—White Leader)

R.S.A. 100 *words a minute, Easter,* 1967 (I)

There is nothing new, of course, in the discovery that / small
children will try to smoke and that they think / it a matter of
pride to do so. Smoking is / like wearing long trousers in boys or
50 putting up hair / in girls: it is a sign of growing up. But / the inquiry that has been made into children's smoking habits / at a
school in the Midlands reveals a most depressing / picture. What
is new, not to say shocking, is to / find the smoking habit being
formed by children as young / as five, and worse still, to learn of

34

parents who / actually take pride in it. No child of five can / be   100
said to be grown-up in any sense of / the word but they quite
naturally imitate their elders and / there seems no harm in their
buying sweet cigarettes and / indulging in other harmless imita-
tions of their parents. When, however, / the extent of the prob-   150
lem becomes apparent, in that forty / per cent of these children
are said to be smoking / at the age of fourteen, the outlook is very
disturbing. /

It is common enough for parents to remain indifferent to /
their children's behaviour. There are always those who feel that /   200
the discipline of their children is someone else's job. The / increase
in child crime is the result. But approval of / a child's early addic-
tion to tobacco is very difficult to / explain. If such parents take
pride in the formation of / the habit, before whom is it displayed?
It is an / odd thought that relatives should not raise an occasional   250
protest / at the encouragement of this vice. Many parents are
ignorant / of the physical harm smoking will do to their children /
but perhaps the greatest harm of all stems from the / general
atmosphere which allows it at all in the young. /   300

(*Shorthand of this passage is on p.* 105)

PASSAGE G (Tape 4—White Leader)

R.S.A. 100 *words a minute, Easter*, 1967 (II)

Everybody talks about Great Britain's foreign trade problem
and how / we are continually importing more than we are exporting but / very few appear to understand the way in which the /
foreign exchange rates actually work.

The rate of exchange between / two currencies has an important function to perform; that is / to balance the purchasing   50
power of the currencies over the / goods of their respective countries. As an example, if sterling / is over-valued on the exchanges
in terms of dollars, / British goods will be too dear in comparison
with American / goods. In other words, the British would be
offering too / little and demanding too much in terms of goods   100
for / the Americans to trade with us. It is true that / for a time
America would increase her exports to us / because she could sell
here at lower prices than would / pay the home producer. But in   130
the course of a / short time, the increased demand for dollars on   150
the part / of British importers and the reduced supply of dollars

35

resulting / from diminished British exports would reduce the flow
of American / exports to Britain. In the long run, an inappropriate
200 rate / of exchange reduces the flow of trade in both directions. /

(*Shorthand of this passage is on p.* 106)

PASSAGE H (Tape 4—White Leader)
R.S.A. 100 *words a minute, Easter,* 1967 (III)

All the signs are that this year's annual meeting of / the International Association for Science will be the most critical / in its
long history. It is strange that financial troubles / should over-
shadow the future of this international institution at / a time
50 when the need for more general understanding of / science is
urgent.

As the boundaries of science advance, the / Association's role
has become more and more exacting. In the / past it has been
criticized for its failure to deal / with current problems. Much
has now been done to remedy / this weakness of being remote
100 from life in the modern / world. This year's programme includes
discussions of current public interest / such as the testing of drugs.
Surely there is no / topic more in the public eye than this. Similarly problems / connected with high-speed transport are a matter
of the / greatest public interest with aircraft now travelling well
150 beyond the / speed of sound. Nor should it fail to provide those /
concerned with planning with helpful indications of the results of /
research. Scientists, of course, turn to specialized meetings for
keeping / abreast of developments in their field, but here as no-
where / else perhaps, the Association provides centres for discus-
200 sion by experts / on matters of general concern.

What is less appreciated is / the considerable effort put into
arranging lectures between the annual / meetings. To these lectures
audiences of nearly three hundred thousand / were attracted last
year with young people well represented.

All / this costs money and it is particularly unfortunate that
250 the / Association should run into financial difficulties just when
it has / begun to equip itself for its proper function in the / field
of science communication. The Association is highly regarded
abroad / as a leading body in its special field of activity. / A fur-
300 ther reduction of its valuable activities should not happen. /

(*Shorthand of this passage is on p.* 107)

R.S.A. 100 *words a minute, Whitsun,* 1967 (I)

The number of deaths arising from road accidents during the / first two days of the August Bank holiday weekend fell / this year compared with the same period last year. On / Sunday, however, there was an increase of seven in the / number of fatal accidents compared with the same day of **/** the previous year. Provisional   50 figures issued by the Ministry of / Transport show that by mid-   60 night on Sunday, deaths for the / first three days of the holiday reached sixty-two.

The / figures, however, are not very revealing. It would be more / to the point if the parts of the country in **/** which the accidents   100 occurred were indicated together with the causes / of each acci- dent. Were bad roads the main cause? Which / type of road user   120 was to blame? Were most of / the accidents in daylight or dark-   130 ness? These are some of / the questions to which answers would be helpful. The road **/** safety problem requires more analysis if   150 any appreciable reduction in / the number of fatalities is to be achieved.

It is / true most road users behave sensibly and this is shown / by the fact that the number of fatal accidents is / just about the same as it was thirty years ago. **/**   200

(*Shorthand of this passage is on p.* 108)

R.S.A. 100 *words a minute, Whitsun,* 1967 (II)

Many of the owners of small businesses would confirm that / there are disadvantages in being part of a large business / organi- zation whereas to be independent is very satisfying. Despite this, / however, there is a clear trend towards the development of / larger and larger units in many sections of this country's **/** life. It is be-   50 coming increasingly true of the British textile / industry. The smaller manufacturers are not at all happy about / their future prospects over the next five or six years. / The credit squeeze has reduced their profits to such an / extent as to make production barely worth while. The prices **/** of their shares on the Stock Ex-   100 change have fallen cutting / off enormous amounts from their capital value. As a consequence / of these and other factors the small family businesses are / beginning to ask themselves whether the price they pay for / their independence is really justified. The

37

150 idea of amalgamation is **/** in the air and again rumours of mergers are to / be heard everywhere. In fact many people are reminded of / the year nineteen sixty-four when so many of the / smaller firms were swallowed up as a result of amalgamation. /

200 Yet some of the smaller concerns are still highly profitable. **/** In some cases their profits have risen year after year / giving a splendid return on the capital which has been / invested. The secret of their success is often to be / found in the fact that they have been able to / attach themselves to a very large and successful

250 retailing organization. **/** When a manufacturer supplies a store with a national reputation / which has branches all over the country its marketing problems / are over. It means he can work to steady and / continuous production schedules. It also means that the quality of / the finished materials can be chosen to suit his

300 requirements. **/**

(*Shorthand of this passage is on p.* 109)

PASSAGE C (Tape 4—Red Leader)

R.S.A. 100 *words a minute, Whitsun,* 1967 (III)

It is surprising how many activities require a licence. They / range from the ownership of a dog to the reception / of television programmes. But the more unusual activities for which / licences are needed are those controlled by the Home Secretary. / They

50 include, for example, the carrying on and supervision of **/** betting shops as well as the right to open cinemas / on Sundays. Many of these regulations are certainly the result / of historical accident. Very frequently they arose from the campaigns / of private Members of Parliament whose high moral motives have / long since

100 been lost in the mists of time. We **/** should ask ourselves what this supervision is intended to achieve / and how far it is successful.

It is true that / some of the more curious provisions of these ancient Acts / of Parliament have recently been abolished but many still remain. / Owners of restaurants who are known to be

150 perfectly respectable **/** are still required to apply for a licence and among / other things swear on oath that water as well as / wine will be available to their customers. Taxi-drivers in / London still operate under a regulation which requires them to / carry hay for

200 the refreshment of their horses. How far **/** is the machinery for controlling the sale of wines and / spirits tending to prevent supermarkets from entering this field? In **/** the same way it is extremely difficult for newcomers to / break into the licensed public house

38

trade. How far do / these ancient controls prevent change? Many
controls are, of course, / necessary to protect the public and at   250
first most of / the legislation was based on good grounds. But we
must / be careful to ensure that when conditions change then our /
laws change with them. We must not allow licensing to / result
in such rigidity that all change is continually stifled. /   300

(Shorthand of this passage is on p. 110)

240.

9/61

mins.

PASSAGE D (Tape 4—Red Leader)

80.
100:

R.S.A. 100 *words a minute, Autumn,* 1968 (I)

   It is probably a fair statement to say that when / a young person leaves school he has three courses of / action open to him. In
the first place he can / obtain a job, secondly he can secure a post
which / involves some sort of training as an apprentice, or he / can   50
begin preparing for a profession.
   The first possibility is / filled with danger for it could be anything from a / job in the Civil Service to washing down cars at /
the local garage. At the one extreme it could be / an occupation
without a future and at the other it / could be a satisfying and   100
well-rewarded post filled with / interest. It is an unfortunate fact
of life that jobs / are divided into those which are socially acceptable, such as / working in an office, and those which seemingly
offer no / clear prospects of advancement. There is no doubt that
with / careful and tactful guidance, a number of the less socially /   150
acceptable jobs between the ages of sixteen and nineteen would /
clarify a young person's ideas about the sort of career / he would
like to undertake. Few middle-class parents would / seriously consider such a course of action. Even working-class / parents fail   200
to see advantages in such a choice.
   Consequently / there is tremendous pressure to obtain jobs
which carry status, / even though they are often the most frustrat-
ing for in / every government department and commercial organization the barriers to advancement / exist even if they are difficult
to describe. Frequently they / involve habits of speech or customs   250
of behaviour. On the / other hand they may be related to membership of a / club or a particular group.   275

(Shorthand of this passage is on p. 111)

240.
(2.4)

PASSAGE E (Tape 4—Red Leader)

R.S.A. 100 *words a minute, Autumn,* 1968 (II)

A statement which is frequently repeated is that this country /
must export if it is to survive. It is therefore / somewhat alarming
to read in a recent report on exporting / to the United States that
British exporters are by no / means as aware of opportunities in
50   that country as we / would imagine.

In particular, the report does not accept that / major industries
such as tourism or the export of machinery / are as fully exploited
as they could be. The fashionable / idea that the biggest opportunities rest with the small firms / and the minor industries is
100 wrong. If the products are / successful in the export market some
small firms are often / unable to produce them in sufficient
quantities. On the contrary, / says the report, the immediate
opportunity for growth lies with / the large industries and the
big firms, of which only / a very few are now doing a professional
150 job of / marketing in the United States.

One of the greatest obstacles / is the shortage of men with
university training in business / management. The old, as well as
the new universities are / making special efforts to remedy this
deficiency but greater concentration / of money on fewer institu-
200 tions might result in an increased / flow of able young men to fill
these positions. Britain / has much to learn from the Japanese,
225 who have studied / the best American marketing techniques. /

(*Shorthand of this passage is on p.* 112)

PASSAGE F (Tape 4—Red Leader)

R.S.A. 100 *words a minute, Autumn,* 1968 (III)

Most of us as private citizens are not directly concerned / with
large sums of money and the buying of a / house is probably the
biggest and most important financial transaction / in which we
are involved. In view of the great / importance of this act it is
50   surprising how few use / the services of an insurance broker in
obtaining the necessary / finance. It becomes all the more surprising when it is / realized that these services are quite free to
the borrower. /

A good insurance broker knows where money is available at /
100 any given time, knowledge which may save the applicant much /
wasted time and effort in fruitless approaches to a series / of
different institutions. The broker will also know whether the /

money is available for the type of property the house-/hunter has in mind. Also the broker can advise the / applicant whether he can really afford to buy the type / of house he wants. In fact, there is a lot / to be said for enlisting the broker's aid long before / the actual purchase of a house. A young married man, / for instance, who expects to buy a house in several / years' time can have his budget worked out in advance. / This would indicate the approximate price range within which he / will have to seek his house and the most suitable / arrangements he can make to build up the necessary deposit / with the minimum of financial stress.

Some brokers operate a / regular monthly subscription plan, the proceeds of which are divided / between a savings account with a building society, and a / life assurance policy which can be used to pay off / the outstanding balance of the mortgage if the husband should / die. The savings with the building society go towards the / deposit as well as giving first call on their funds. /

150

200

250

300

(*Shorthand of this passage is on p.* 113)

PASSAGE G (Tape 4—Red Leader)

R.S.A. 100 *words a minute, Whitsun,* 1969 (I)

At the beginning of this century the average man could / just about expect to reach fifty years of age, and / only a generation ago the number of people who became / sixty-five was not significant. Most children living today, together / with a good percentage of their parents, can expect to / attain eighty and even ninety years. This is about ten / years more than the present average. Many doctors who specialize / in the problem of ageing feel that an average life / span of one hundred years is in sight. That more / people do not reach a century seems to stem from / the fact that they are unable or unwilling to follow / a system of proper diet coupled with controlled exercise and / rest. It goes without saying that we must be moderate / in all we do.

The widely held view that people / just get old and die is obsolete, for attempts to / find just one person who has died merely of old / age have proved unsuccessful. No one has ever been found / who died what might be called a completely natural death / in the sense that their body expired because it was / too old. Deterioration is not due to the passage of / time but is really the result of disease of some / kind. If any single process is responsible for ageing, science / has not yet learned what it is.

50

100

150

200

41

There is no / doubt that the physical make-up which we inherit
250 from / our parents plays an important part in the length of / our
life because individuals seem to have different rates of / living.
People seem to burn themselves out at different speeds. / Our
surroundings, too, affect this aspect of getting old. For / example,
experiments show that rats kept in cool conditions live / longer
than rats kept at room temperature.
300 Very recent findings / seem to indicate that life can retain its
vigour. Doctors / are not agreed how long we might live if we /
were completely free from illness or accident but a theoretical /
figure of over one hundred and twenty-five years has / been sug-
350 gested. What would we do with the extra years? /

(*Shorthand of this passage is on p.* 114)

PASSAGE H (Tape 4—Red Leader)
R.S.A. 100 *words a minute, Whitsun,* 1969 (II)

In contrast to some other countries, Britain's students, although
not / well treated, are quite well-off particularly when compared
with / their opposite numbers in France. But they share one
grievance / that is common to all students today. They are no /
50 longer prepared to accept the curious status of being halfway /
between a child and an adult. When it is a / matter of study they
are expected to think and act / like an adult but in matters of
discipline and the / organization of the college they are treated
like children.
This / presents a major challenge to universities. Can they
100 satisfy the / desire of students for a voice in the arranging of / the
university's affairs without loss in the standard of the / education
which they offer? The issue offers a challenge to / the students as
much as to the teachers. If they / wish to be treated as adults,
150 adult conduct is indispensable. /

(*Shorthand of this passage is on p.* 115)

PASSAGE I (Tape 4—Red Leader)
R.S.A. 100 *words a minute, Autumn,* 1969 (III)

Christmas is the time of the year when big stores / cover their
counters with displays of magnificent gifts. It is / also the period
of the year when the number of / cases of theft rises by about

fifty per cent. New / efforts to protect the stores and combat shop-lifting are **/** now being introduced some of which use the most modern / equipment.   50

In the face of increasing loss from theft it / is natural to employ extra staff on security duties and / to increase safeguards like spot checks on employees leaving the / premises, but some stores are going much farther than this. **/** A shop in the suburbs   100 of London was losing over / one hundred pounds a week through shop-lifting and finally / decided to install an American device at a cost of / over five thousand pounds. It paid for itself within a / year. The device consisted of an invisible beam which was **/**   150 placed at the exit of the store. Each garment in / the shop had a metal price tag attached to it / and when the article was sold the assistant tore off / the metallic portion of the price ticket. A shop-lifter / who hid the garment in a bag, or tried to **/** walk out   200 wearing it, had to pass through the invisible / beam which warned the security staff.

Several stores are using / a new device to help them in tracing people who / pass worthless cheques. In this case there is a hidden / camera at the cashier's desk which automatically takes a photograph **/** of both the customer and the cheque. The film is /   250 developed only if the cheque is not met and the / police are provided with a very simple method of identifying / the person concerned. The introduction of these and other new / methods of detection makes petty thieving more and more difficult. **/**   300

(*Shorthand of this passage is on p.* 116)

PASSAGE A (Tape 5—White Leader)

R.S.A. 120 *words a minute, Summer,* 1966 (I)

I like my neighbour's apples better than any others. They / come off a tree which overhangs our garden fence. He / allows us to pick the apples, and in return we / do not fuss about the branches of his tree keeping / the sun off our flowers. Strictly, that tree has no **/** business to extend beyond the edge of our neighbour's property. / It is a nuisance, in law, and we are entitled / to   50 have the branches off.

Shade from an overhanging branch / may be pleasant, but water from a defective gutter is / another thing. Yet, in law, they can both amount to **/** the same kind of nuisance, and you can have   100 them / stopped. The same rules apply, for example, to the roots / of a tree which extend into your land from your / neighbour's garden and damage the foundations of your house.

43

150   While / it is true that the law allows you to apply / your own remedy, quite how far this permission goes is / not easy to say. One thing is clear: that if / you do more damage to your neighbour's property than is / really necessary to get rid of a nuisance,

200   then he / can make you liable. So, if you are wise, you / will ask him to deal with the trouble. To do / this you need not wait until the water is actually / coming through your walls; the mere fact that his gutter / overhangs your land may give you the right to

250   have / it removed. Indeed, you must not wait too long without / protesting, or he may, over the years, acquire a permanent / right to leave matters as they are. If you have / trouble with things encroaching on your land, I advise you / to give your neighbour a chance to put them right; / and if he does not, ask advice from a

300   solicitor / or a citizens' advice bureau.

      As regards the garden fences, / sometimes it is difficult to know who owns which fence. / You may find the answer in the title deeds of / your house, but if not you have to look further / afield.

350   What about the simple test of looking at the / fence and seeing which side the posts are on? Most / people want to put a fence on the very edge / of their land. They can only do this if they / put the posts on their own side, as otherwise the / posts would be on

400   their neighbour's land. This, however, is / no more than a rough and ready rule.

      Even when / you cannot make your neighbour mend his fence, you are / not quite powerless. An encroaching fence is on the same / legal footing as an overhanging tree. The law calls them / nuisances,

450   and will help you to get rid of them. /

(*Shorthand of this passage is on p.* 117)

PASSAGE B (Tape 5—White Leader)

R.S.A. 120 *words a minute, Summer,* 1966 (II)

      The Chairman said: Your board has for some years past / followed a generous dividend policy and intends to continue to / do so to the extent that future profits, the effect / of the revised basis of company taxation and the general / requirements of the business permit.

50   It is apt to record / here that your company has not called upon shareholders or / the market for additional capital during the past twenty-five / years, and during that time the business has been financed / out of our own resources, supplemented by normal bank facilities. /

It is my view that in practice, when the full / effects of the   100
increased tax burden are felt, a number / of adverse tendencies
will result. The changes must, I feel, / act against the expansion
of business and the modernization of / plant, machinery and
methods. It is essential, if British industry / is to remain competitive both at home and abroad, and / keep its costs down to   150
minimum levels, that as little / limitation as possible should be
placed upon its ability to / keep up to date and take the fullest
advantage of / technical advances. We feel that enterprise should
not be curbed. /

During the year under review our canning turnover showed a /   200
slight decrease, but on the other hand there was a / marked improvement in our sales of frozen food. In this / latter section of
our business, turnover has grown by rather / more than sixty per
cent over the last three financial / years, and I am confident that
this trend will continue. /   250

We continue to face intense competition in both sections of /
our business, but this is particularly so on the canned / goods
side, where over-production has taken place generally throughout /
the trade during the twelve months under review.

We are / continually striving to improve our methods and there-
by to reduce / our costs, and in this connection we invested dur-   300
ing the / last twelve months some two hundred and thirty thousand pounds / on production and distribution facilities.

Both management and staff at / all levels fully recognize the
need for a critical attitude / to current methods and the necessity
of continuous change if / progress is to be won. The food trade   350
and the / housewife recognize that our brand guarantees the highest
quality, and / I would like to add that at no time have / our prices
been more competitive than at present. Since June, / a year ago,
we have reduced the price of fifty-/three and held the price of   400
seventy-seven sizes of / canned products out of a total of one
hundred and / fifty. If account is taken of the increase in labour /
and other costs it will be realized that this present / policy was not
effected without effort.

We continue to make / steady progress with our export trade;   450
and we are making / particular efforts in North America. We did
not achieve as / much as we had hoped, notably in Africa, owing
to / the suddenly imposed import restrictions. All our agents and
customers / throughout the world have been visited as is our   500
usual / custom, and prospects for the future appear to be good. /   510

(*Shorthand of this passage is on p.* 118)

45

R.S.A. 120 *words a minute, Autumn,* 1966 (I)

    In modern offices women tend to get about twenty per / cent less space than men doing similar work, according to / a study by the Building Research Station. It seems that / the more space an office worker needs the less he / tends to get, says the survey. The
50 principal scientific officer **/** at the station makes the comment that "high status and / membership of the male sex is a better guarantee of / good accommodation than the requirements of the job." He goes / on to say that a study of offices in and / around
100 the City of London showed that only four per **/** cent of the premises visited had any special arrangements for / drying wet clothes, only twenty-three per cent provided rest / rooms in spite of a greater number of female staff, / and but six per cent had a canteen or some / other facilities for the provision of meals.
150   Another survey showed **/** that of two thousand modern offices, only a third provided / a locker or cupboard for hats and coats, and fewer / than two-thirds a place in which personal belongings could / be locked up. Forty per cent of the occupants of / office
200 buildings found their offices too hot in summer. About **/** fifty per cent of the staff complained that their offices / were stuffy in both summer and winter. A problem in / modern buildings arises from the large windows and lightly clad / walls that allow too much
240 noise to enter the building. /

(*Shorthand of this passage is on p.* 120)

R.S.A. 120 *words a minute, Autumn,* 1966 (II)

    Although most people think of animal air-freight in terms / of a pet dog being flown to a new home, / or the occasional lion to a zoo, some airlines actually / carry more animals than people. In fact, nearly a million / creatures passed through London Airport
50 last year. The traffic flows **/** as regularly as the tides, and without it many commercial / concerns would be under a grave handicap.
    These living cargoes / have given airlines a new set of problems; and close / attention to the smallest details is necessary for the safety / and welfare of the animals.
100   To handle the traffic at **/** London Airport there is a special hostel run by The / Royal Society for the Prevention of Cruelty to Animals, where / all kinds of living creatures can be rested,

cleaned and / fed between flights, or while awaiting collection.
Since opening in / nineteen hundred and fifty-two, the hostel has
housed nearly **/** seven million animals. Each guest has its own   150
diet, so / that every type of food has to be stocked in / the larder.
One awkward guest was a large sea elephant / which devoured sixteen pounds of herring at a sitting.

   The / airlines go to great trouble to satisfy individual needs, as **/** 200
well as those of the dealers who provide the traffic. /   210

   (Shorthand of this passage is on p. 120)

PASSAGE E (Tape 5—White Leader)

R.S.A. 120 *words a minute, Summer,* 1968 (II)

   If you run out of cheques there is nothing to / stop you from
writing one on anything. The laws relating / to cheques date back
to 1882, where it / is laid down that a twopenny stamp must be
affixed / to make a cheque legal. Whether you use a normal **/**   50
cheque form or a scrap of paper, there are certain / responsibilities
you have when you write out a cheque, although / most of them
rest on the bank's shoulders.

   A cheque / is an undertaking by the bank's customer (the
drawer of / the cheque) that the sum involved will be handed
over **/** by the bank on presentation of the cheque. This does / not   100
mean that the bank is obliged to pay out / if the customer has no
money in his account and / no overdraft facility.

   On the other hand, if Brown writes / a cheque in favour of
Jones, and the bank stops **/** the cheque by mistake, Jones cannot   150
sue the bank but / could sue Brown. The bank could be sued by
Brown / if he thought his reputation damaged.

   The drawer has a / duty to take reasonable care to prevent
forgery. If a / bank pays out against a forged cheque, it is just **/**   200
bad luck. The drawer might have to bear the loss / if he filled in
his cheque in a negligent manner / so that the sum could be
altered, either because there / were spaces or because the writing
could be changed. If / you should lose your cheque book you
should tell the **/** bank at once because the bank and not you   250
would / suffer if the cheques were used.

   The crossed cheque has / become the more common form, as
people have learnt that / an uncrossed cheque is dangerous. If
you write out an / uncrossed cheque to John Smith and he loses
it, the **/** finder merely endorses the cheque, that is, signs the   300
name / "John Smith" on the back and cashes it without being /

traced. A crossed cheque must be paid into somebody's
account /— it can never be exchanged for cash at a bank. /
350   To avoid a crossed cheque being endorsed in favour of / somebody other than the person you intended to pay you / write "a/c
payee only" between the crossings. You could take / this precau-
tion if you were paying your landlord through a / not too honest
estate agent. It would stop the agent / paying the cheque into his
400 own account (intending to pay / your landlord later) and remove
any fears you might have / about his defaulting.
    Suppose you make out a crossed cheque / to John Smith. He
endorses it but loses the cheque. / The finder cashes it at a public
house pretending to / be John Smith. As the publican has taken
450 the cheque / in good faith, you would have to honour it
although / John Smith lost it. To avoid this sort of thing / you
should always write "not negotiable" between the crossings.
    Finally, / a crossed cheque on which is written "pay cash" is /
500 called an open crossed cheque, and can only be cashed / at a bank
510 by the drawer or his known agent. /

(*Shorthand of this passage is on p.* 121)

PASSAGE F (Tape 5—White Leader)

R.S.A. 120 *words a minute, Easter* 1967 (I)

    It is not life but essay competitions that have made / me think
about old age. I acted as judge in / one such competition, and I
have been running a small / one in this village, the subject being
"What old people / need." Nearly all the little pieces have been
50   written by / women. All of them mentioned the usual things —
a room / of their own, warmth, and an occasional visitor — but
several / of them added that they needed to be needed. Surely / it
is too often forgotten that the old can give / as well as take.
100   Many of our arrangements cut the / lifeline between the old
and the very young. There can / be a fine relationship between
the sevens and the seventy-/fives. They are both closer to the
world of myth / and magic than all the people in between those
150 ages. / When I was very young we had my grandmother living /
with us, and, whenever my parents went out for the / evening,
she fed and entertained me. After we had eaten / our rice pudding,
she told me about the daily life / and customs in the West Riding
well over a century / ago. Even twenty teachers could not have

48

given me as / much as she did — in quantity, yes, but not in /   200
quality. What was there was the magic that begins with / experience and needs an outlook close to wonder and far / from worry,
often common to childhood and to old age. /

It is chiefly the humbler old folk who are ready /to write little   250
pieces saying what they need. It is / this humility that prevents
them from saying outright what I /think is implied in their pieces;
and as they won't / say it, then I, one of them, will say it / for
them. In spite of all this "Problem of the / Aged" stuff, and all   300
the arrangements and possible arrangements of / the national and
local societies, this is not by any / means a good world in which
to reach old age. /   330

(*Shorthand of this passage is on p.* 123)

PASSAGE G (Tape 5—White Leader)

R.S.A. 120 *words a minute, Easter,* 1967 (II)

Among the people who live near you or work with / you there
are certain to be many who have a / bank account. Possession of
an account does not mean that / these people are better off than
you. It simply means / that they accept banking for what it is: a
service / which today exists for the benefit of everyone. In con-   50
sequence, / they have no more hesitation about using the services
of / a bank than they have about entering a post office. /

A bank gives the same service to every customer, without /
regard to the size of the account. The facilities it / provides can   100
be used by everyone who likes to keep / money matters in order --
and that, almost certainly, includes you. /   120

(*Shorthand of this passage is on p.* 124)

PASSAGE H (Tape 5—White Leader)

R.S.A. 120 *words a minute, Easter,* 1967 (III)

It has been said often enough that local government offers /
not one career but a great many, and a recent / survey has shown
how large the number really is. The / occupations now to be
found in the service, from accountant / to youth officer, add up
to well over six hundred. / Some of these could hardly be called   50
career jobs, but / in about a quarter of them a young man or / a
young woman could find enough of a challenge and / reward to
satisfy the highest ambition.

The cities and larger / counties are responsible for the whole
100   range of public services **/** coming under local administration in
their areas, and they are / therefore able to offer a wide choice of
work to / anyone who wishes to make local government a career.
There / is a widely held notion that "working for the council"/
150   must be dull. This is, of course, quite untrue, for **/** the local authorities must have more than their share of / jobs with endless interest
and variety. Above all, in these / days there is a demand for people
with drive and / ambition who have the ability to grasp facts
quickly and / think along logical lines. They could be the top
200   people **/** of the next ten years, because movement and promotion
may / be swift for the most able.
Men who have had / a few years' experience since qualifying
are required in particular / to cope with the growing circle of
activities in the / professional and technical fields. Careers of
250   much interest are offered, **/** for example, in connection with roads,
bridges, etc., and to / cope with the ever-growing traffic problem
on the roads. /
Local authorities have not been slow to see the value / of
mechanization. Their adoption of the newest methods for carry-
300   ing / out both the most routine and the most complicated tasks **/**
is creating a demand for suitable candidates, both men and /
women, to train as operators. For persons suited to this / kind of
work an exciting career is thrown open in / most of the larger
authorities.
When careers are written about / there is a tendency to show
350   what is on offer **/** to young men, and to mention young women
only as / though in afterthought. Indeed the number of young
women who / remain in the service and rise to responsible posts
is / small. The service does, however, highly value the contribution
400   of / women in two fields – the social services and in typing **/** and
machine operation. In the expanding health, welfare and children's **/**
services there are good openings for the young woman with / a
bent for social work. Training is now given to / those selected;
and the return of women who qualified before / marriage but
450   later find it possible to resume their career **/** in one of the social
services, is welcomed. Despite the / appearance of the audio typing
pool, shorthand-typists are still / very much in demand to fill the
posts of secretary / to senior officials.
Those starting on a career or wishing / to change their jobs can
500   look to local government to **/** provide worthwhile posts in the
510   service of the community. /

(*Shorthand of this passage is on p.* 125)

PASSAGE A (Tape 5—Red Leader)

R.S.A. 120 *words a minute, Whitsun,* 1967 (I)

Why does a dog wag his tail? The right answer / is simple. Wagging his tail is the only way the / dog can express goodwill to others at the most critical / moments of his life, when it may be a matter / of life or death to him.

Watch two dogs approaching / each other in the open, when   50
neither is sure whether / the other is friend or enemy. They walk on wires. / The hair stands up stiffly on their necks. Every muscle / in their bodies is tense with readiness, and both are / growling. They walk round and round each other, and the / way each one   100
tries to seem grand without provoking the / other too far is laughable. Neither really wants to fight, / but how can they let each other know? They dare / not relax a muscle, because the fight may come about / after all. What are they to do?

Happily nature never / leaves her creatures without some way   150
out of the ordinary / difficulties of their lives. Every dog has his tail, which / is the *only* part of himself that the animal can / move without injuring his chances in a fight. So nature, / always helpful in all creatures, has given to the whole / dog tribe the instinct to   200
use their tails to signal / goodwill to one another. Watching the two I have referred / to while they are still walking round each other, you / may see a gentle movement of the tail of one / of them. Looking at the other you observe that his / tail is slightly   250
wagging too. In less than a minute / they will be playing together.

So, because, in the great / crises of his life the dog has no other means / of expressing good feeling, he has acquired the habit of / wagging his tail whenever he feels pleased or good-tempered. /   300

(*Shorthand of this passage is on p.* 126)

PASSAGE B (Tape 5—Red Leader)

R.S.A. 120 *words a minute, Whitsun,* 1967 (II)

It comes as a surprise to many people that there / are thousands of large wild animals free to wander in / Britain. There are probably more wild deer here today than / there were four centuries ago. Even more surprising is how / little we see of them, though they do come into / towns if gardens offer meals.   50

In earlier times many deer / were animals of forest and woodland, and when these were / reduced some, like the red deer, took

51

to the hills. / Now, because of the 1963 Deer Act and / increased
100 tree planting, they are making a return that presents **/** some
problems.

Not all the deer we may see are / true natives. Some have been
introduced or have established themselves / after escaping from
the parks of stately homes.

Possibly the / most striking feature of the deer is the antlers
150 that / often seem to outweigh the head of the mature stag. **/**

(*Shorthand of this passage is on p.* 127)

PASSAGE C (Tape 5—Red Leader)
R.S.A. 120 *words a minute, Whitsun,* 1967 (III)

The Chairman said: The financial year, the results of which /
are now before you, has been a year of change / within your company. This change includes a complete review of / management
with the object of obtaining an increase in production. /
50 We have introduced management accounting to enable us to
control **/** costs in a more effective way. This should help us / in
our decisions with regard to future improvements.

Our arrangements / for dealing with industrial relations and
work study have been / made stronger. Our aim here is by a
thorough examination / of our working methods to bring about
100 changes which will **/** benefit both the company and its employees.

We have for / a long time been looking into the merits of a /
computer system for accounting purposes and also for providing
statistics / in connection with our operations. The computer has
150 been installed / at our new offices and is now in full operation. **/**

There is no doubt that these new facilities will be / of great
importance in supplying us with the increased amount / of information that is necessary for modern management. It is / a question
not only of providing information more cheaply but / also of
200 enabling us to receive it much more quickly, **/** and this again
improves management control.

Of course, changes of / this kind entail a temporary increase in
the costs of / administration, but I am sure that the money has
been / well spent and will prove its worth in terms of / increased
profit in the years to come.
250 For some years **/** now we have felt an increasing lack of space
at / our head offices, and it has been clear that we / should have
to secure larger premises elsewhere. The question has / been ex-
amined in all its aspects, and it was decided / some time ago to

move the major part of our **/** offices to a suburb of London where   300
a lease has / been arranged for a new office building. Space has
been / obtained at a much lower rent than we should have / had
to pay in London, and at the same time / it will now be possible
for the majority of our **/** head office staff to reach their place of   350
work in / much less time and with much less effort than before. /

We have found it essential that our sales department should /
remain in London, and a number of the company's senior / officers
also need a London office. We have therefore taken **/** the lease of   400
a small office building in the Victoria / area; and our present
building has been placed in the / market. A notice of the change
has been sent to / all concerned.

I pointed out in my statement last year / that the company's
production facilities were stretched to the limit, **/** and this situa-   450
tion has continued throughout the year. Our sales / show an increase of two per cent, but we have / been unable to increase output to the same extent. When / considering the future, however,
I have no doubt that the / demand will continue to rise and that
your company will **/** be able to meet its share of the increased   500
sales. /   510

(Shorthand of this passage is on p. 128)

PASSAGE D (Tape 5—Red Leader)

R.S.A. 120 *words a minute, Autumn,* 1967 (I)

In this bank we do not just offer you a / job, but a career. It
is a career that requires / intelligence and integrity, and the ability
to make friends and / get on well with people; a career that puts
you / in the centre of local life.

We run a complete **/** training scheme for our new entrants.   50
You will be able / to attend special courses on practical banking
at our Staff / Training Centres. If you come straight from school,
you will / be granted leave during the day to prepare for the /
examinations of the Institute of Bankers.

The prospects are good. **/** The salaries of branch managers   100
range from over two thousand / pounds to around five thousand   110
pounds, and there are opportunities / for advancement with   120
greater rewards.

The bank believes in friendly / relations among the staff and
with its customers. After hours, / we are just as friendly too.
The bank club boasts **/** a wide range of activities, not only in   150

53

sport but / in a host of other interests. There are special benefits / for the staff, such as help in buying a house; / and there is a good pension on retirement.

200   If you / wish to know more about a career in the bank, / you
210   should contact the Staff Manager at our London office. /

(Shorthand of this passage is on p. 130)

PASSAGE E (Tape 5—Red Leader)

R.S.A. 120 *words a minute, Autumn,* 1969 (I)

In the part of Australia where I grew up we / used to come across snakes quite often when we were / walking in the bush, and our fear and loathing of / them was something more than the
50   usual thing, mainly, I / suppose, because very occasionally some of us really did get / bitten. I never saw a snake — that furtive sliminess, that / mad, hating eye — without a sudden instinctive constriction of the / heart, and after the first moment of panic was over / we children had just one thought in our minds: "Kill /
100   it. Do not let it get away." And so we / would grab a stick and in a spasm of furious / terror we would beat at the hideous twisting thing until / at last it lay inert in the dust. Even then / we would not dare to touch it; we would hook / it up with the stick and toss
150   it away out / of sight into the long grass where ants were bound / to demolish it within a day or two.

We all / knew what to do if we got bitten, and most / of us carried about with us a little tin box / in which were one of
200   father's razor blades and a / phial of permanganate of potash crystals. You tied your handkerchief / round the arm or the leg above the bite and / tightened it by twisting the knot with a
240   piece of / stick. This slowed the flow of poison to the heart. /

(Shorthand of this passage is on p. 130)

PASSAGE F (Tape 5—Red Leader)

R.S.A. 120 *words a minute, Autumn,* 1967 (III)

The Chairman said: As members are aware every five years / there is a valuation of the liabilities in our ordinary / and industrial branches. As last year was the closing year / of the latest period this meeting gives me a suitable / opportunity to take stock of our business and to report / to you on the progress of our efforts.   50

The period / of five years was in some ways a difficult one. / For many years the society had a large house purchase / business. The country's economic difficulties at the beginning of the / period meant that restrictions had to be placed on the / granting   100 of loans for this purpose. At the same time / some of our staff who had relied on this scheme / for a large part of their new business found things / difficult. I am glad to say, however, that although it / has been necessary to restrict this class of business our / staff   150 are now adjusted to the situation.

The other major / event of the period was, of course, the reorganization of / the agency staff which commenced at the beginning of last / year. This change has given rise to a number of / problems which have disturbed the day-to-day working of /   200 the staff in some areas. The scheme is, however, making / good progress. Already over a quarter of our agency staff / are on the new terms and their number is growing / rapidly. The directors are satisfied that the change was a / necessary one and also in the interests of those who / hold our policies.   250

These are two of the difficulties we / have had to contend with in the past five years. / On the other side of the picture has been the / growing earnings in terms of pounds, shillings and pence among / those classes of people with whom we do the bulk / of   300 our business. The general public are becoming aware to / an increasing extent of the advantages of life assurance, and / this is shown by the rapid growth of life assurance / as a whole. It is no doubt a reflection of / the improving standard of living which brings home to the / head of the family the need to provide for his /   350 dependants in the event of his early death.

One aspect / of our business which has given concern to the directors / has been the difficulty of controlling expenses, and it has / been an uphill struggle. Our problem with expenses is the /   400 problem of inflation. Over many of these expenses we have / no control: rents, rates, etc., are examples. These increasing expenses / cannot be met as with other commercial concerns by increasing / the price of our products. The premium for a life / assurance policy is fixed at the outset and cannot be / varied at the wish of   450 the insurance company. The solution / lies in economy of labour and material and in the / expansion of our premium income at a pace which will / enable us to absorb these mounting expenses. One cannot help / but feel, however, that at times we are trying to / stem a tide which it is most difficult to resist. /   510

(*Shorthand of this passage is on p.* 131)

PASSAGE G (Tape 5—Red Leader)

R.S.A. 120 *words a minute, Autumn,* 1968 (I)

When are the rank and file of British offices going / to have
double glazing? In an office I know, if / you open the windows
even a small part of an / inch, you can't hear a word the person at
50   the / other end of the phone is saying. The roar of / the traffic
quite drowns all conversation; and when someone comes /
through the door there is chaos! The draught caused through /
both windows and door being open at the same time / means that
everything in sight flies off the desks.
100   What / some secretaries put up with from 9 a.m. to / 5.30 p.m.
for five days a week is / beyond belief. Small and dark rooms
where you would find / it impossible to swing a cat; bad lighting;
chairs that / lack comfort; desks that ladder their stockings; intense
heat in / the summer and extreme cold in the winter; cloakrooms
150   two / floors below and lifts that seem always to be out / of order.
I wondered how much lack of comfort the / office secretary
could really stand. A good deal, if her / job was interesting, said
the head of one of London's / top employment agencies. Most of
the secretaries I spoke to, / however, did not agree. For them,
200   comfortable office conditions were / just as important as their
salaries. The minimum they think / their due includes a modern
typewriter, a desk of the / right size, with a chair of the right
height; and / a boss who does not lose his temper too often. /
250   If, however, you are a secretary in one of the / many modern
office blocks you can expect a good deal / more. Wall to wall
carpets, modern furniture, a good restaurant / and high speed
lifts. There are other benefits if you / work, for example, in the
offices of an important oil / company in London. These include
300   iced water on every floor, / powder rooms and your own cabinet
in which you can / lock away your personal things. There is also
a left / luggage room for parcels; and a change of air every / four
hours! For leisure time there is a swimming pool, / squash and
badminton courts and a rifle range.
350   At the / head offices of one of the large banks in the / City
of London you pass fountains and flower beds as / you go into
the fine entrance hall, which is all / glass and has modern furniture. The lifts take you to / the twenty-seventh floor in a third
400   of a minute. / The offices are furnished in pastel colours with
fitted carpets / and silk curtains to match. All this luxury does
not / agree with everybody. One secretary said that in the extreme /
450   comfort of her office she found it difficult to concentrate./

(Shorthand of this passage is on p. 133)

R.S.A. 120 *words a minute, Easter,* 1968 (II)

There are somewhere about fourteen million bank accounts
in this / country and I wonder just how many of their owners /
fully realize that, in opening a bank account, they give / their bank
managers full permission to answer any questions about / their
status and their standing in the matter of credit. /   50

The bank managers will answer inquiries only from other bank /
managers. If you want to know what I am worth / you must ask
your bank manager to make a definite / inquiry of my bank
manager: it is no use your / approaching my bank manager direct.

The banks hold that their / right to reply to inquiries about   100
their clients' affairs is / just ordinary business practice and quite
familiar, they claim, to / anyone who opens an account with them.
That I think / is not quite correct or true. I should say that / not
one client in ten knows that his bank manager / answers questions   150
about him or her.

However, the alternative is / very much worse. You can tell
your bank manager not / to answer inquiries about you, and he
will refrain from / doing so; but if someone does inquire and is
told / that your bank manager is not allowed to give any / infor-   200
mation about you, the inquirer's bank manager will interpret that /
as meaning, if not the worst, at the very least / next door to it.

Bank managers communicate with each other / about their
clients in words more or less without meaning / to you and to
me but which are quite clear / if you know the code. They are   250
words that, even / if you got to see them, would certainly not
provide / any sort of basis for resort to legal action.

People / provide bank references either to reassure someone
like a landlord / who may be a little chary whether to accept a /
new tenant, or a business man who is anxious about / credit he is   300
being asked to give. The shorter the / report is the better. The
best description to have made / about oneself is "Undoubted."
Quite satisfactory would be: "Considered good / enough for
your figures and purpose."

It is when the / bank manager adds a number of dependent   350
clauses that the / other bank manager has good cause to feel a
little / worried. Such a phrase as: "Would not enter into a / contract he could not afford" expresses a shade of doubt. / From that
the descent into complete doubt is likely to / be swift. The   400
phrase: "Are rather larger figures than we / are used to" is as near
to: "Look out!" or / "Beware!" as a bank manager will go. After

that the / inquirer is "on his own" and must rely upon his / own judgement.

450   Giving a reference of this kind is not **/** at all an easy job at the best of times. / Difficulties occur for the manager when people have more than / one account and use the smaller one for a reference. / The bank is as a consequence apt to be worried / about

500   being sued either for (without intention) deceiving the man **/** who
510   wants the reference or else for defaming the customer. /

(Shorthand of this passage is on p. 135)

PASSAGE A (Tape 1—White Leader)

R.S.A. 50 *words a minute, Summer,* 1966 (I)

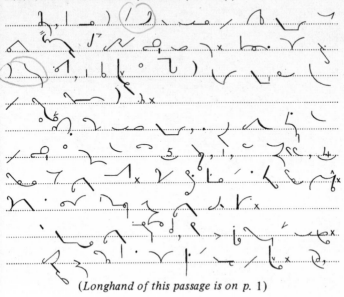

(*Longhand of this passage is on p.* 1)

PASSAGE B (Tape 1—White Leader)

R.S.A. 50 *words a minute, Summer,* 1966 (II)

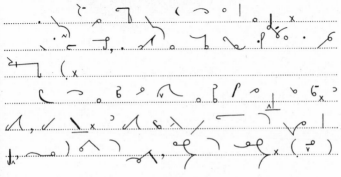

59

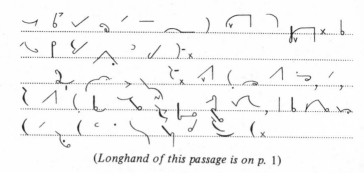

(Longhand of this passage is on p. 1)

PASSAGE C (Tape 1—White Leader)

R.S.A. 50 words a minute, Autumn, 1966 (I)

(Longhand of this passage is on p. 2)

PASSAGE D (Tape 1—White Leader)

R.S.A. 50 words a minute, Autumn, 1966 (II)

(*Longhand of this passage is on p. 2*)

PASSAGE E (Tape 1—White Leader)

R.S.A. 50 words a minute, Easter, 1967 (I)

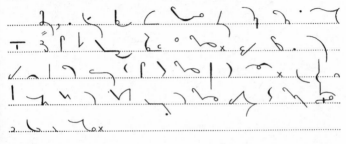

61

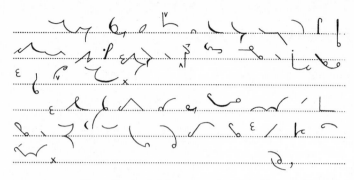

(Longhand of this passage is on p. 3)

PASSAGE F (Tape 1–White Leader)

R.S.A. 50 *words a minute, Easter,* 1967 (II)

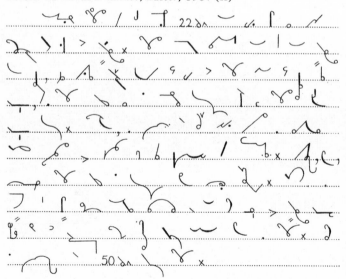

(Longhand of this passage is on p. 3)

PASSAGE G (Tape 1—White Leader)

R.S.A. 50 words a minute, Whitsun, 1967 (I)

(*Longhand of this passage is on p.* 4)

PASSAGE H (Tape 1—White Leader)

R.S.A. 50 words a minute, Whitsun, 1967 (II)

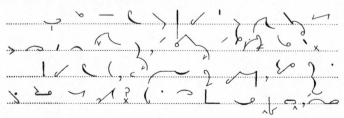

63

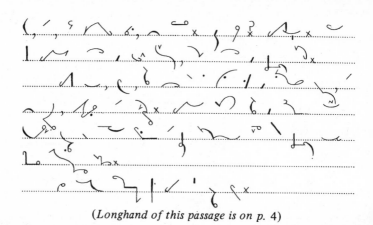

(Longhand of this passage is on p. 4)

PASSAGE A (Tape 1—Red Leader)

R.S.A. 60 words a minute, Summer, 1966 (I)

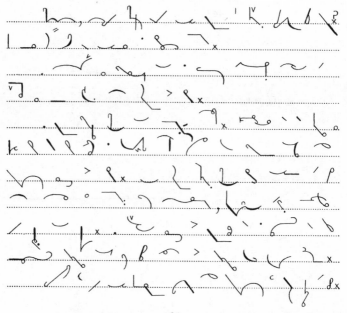

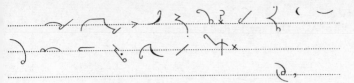

(*Longhand of this passage is on p. 5*)

PASSAGE B (Tape 1—Red Leader)

R.S.A. 60 words a minute, Summer, 1966 (II)

(*Longhand of this passage is on p. 5*)

PASSAGE C (Tape 1—Red Leader)

R.S.A. 60 *words a minute, Autumn,* 1966 (I)

(*Longhand of this passage is on p.* 6)

PASSAGE D (Tape 1—Red Leader)

R.S.A. 60 *words a minute, Autumn,* 1966 (II)

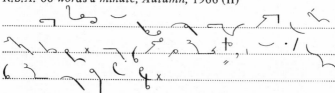

66

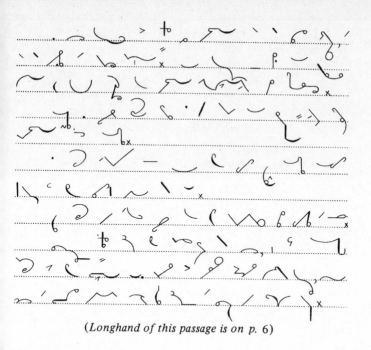

(Longhand of this passage is on p. 6)

PASSAGE E (Tape 1–Red Leader)

R.S.A. 60 *words a minute, Easter,* 1967 (I)

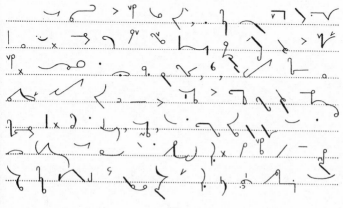

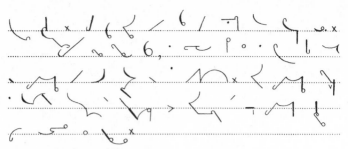

(Longhand of this passage is on p. 7)

PASSAGE F (Tape 1—Red Leader)

R.S.A. 60 *words a minute, Easter,* 1967 (II)

(Longhand of this passage is on p. 8)

PASSAGE G (Tape 1—Red Leader)

R.S.A. 60 words a minute, Whitsun, 1967 (I)

(Longhand of this passage is on p. 8)

PASSAGE H (Tape 1—Red Leader)

R.S.A. 60 words a minute, Whitsun, 1967 (II)

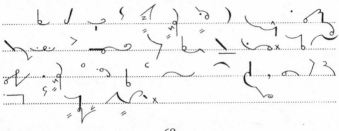

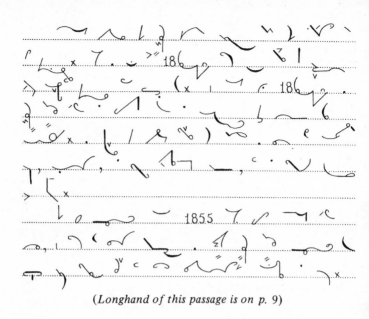

(Longhand of this passage is on p. 9)

PASSAGE A (Tape 2–White Leader)

R.S.A. 80 *words a minute, Summer,* 1966 (I)

(Longhand of this passage is on p. 9)

PASSAGE B (Tape 2—White Leader)

R.S.A. 80 *words a minute, Summer,* 1966 (II)

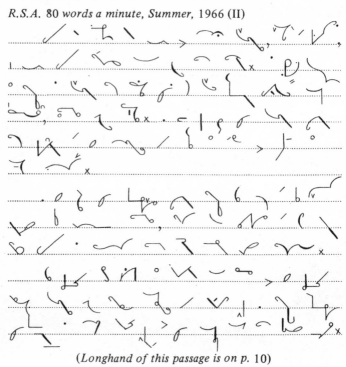

(*Longhand of this passage is on p.* 10)

PASSAGE C (Tape 2—White Leader)

R.S.A. 80 *words a minute, Summer,* 1966 (III)

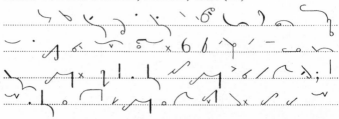

(*Longhand of this passage is on p. 10*)

PASSAGE D (Tape 2—White Leader)

R.S.A. 80 words a minute, Autumn, 1966 (I)

(*Longhand of this passage is on p.* 11)

PASSAGE E (Tape 2—White Leader)

R.S.A. 80 *words a minute, Autumn,* 1966 (II)

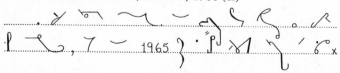

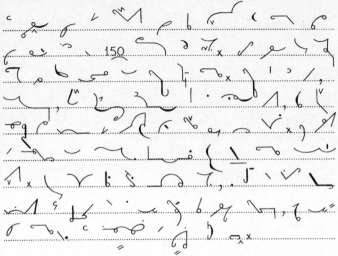

(Longhand of this passage is on p. 12)

PASSAGE F (Tape 2—White Leader)

R.S.A. 80 *words a minute, Autumn,* 1966 (III)

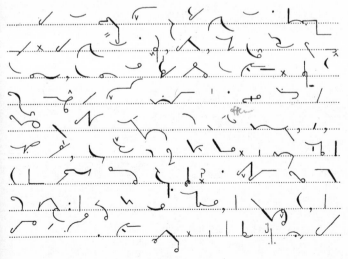

75

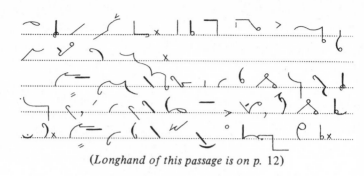

(Longhand of this passage is on p. 12)

PASSAGE G (Tape 2—White Leader)

R.S.A. 80 *words a minute, Easter,* 1967 (I)

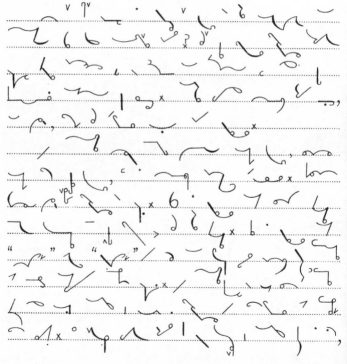

(Longhand of this passage is on p. 13)

PASSAGE H (Tape 2—White Leader)

R.S.A. 80 words a minute, Easter, 1967 (II)

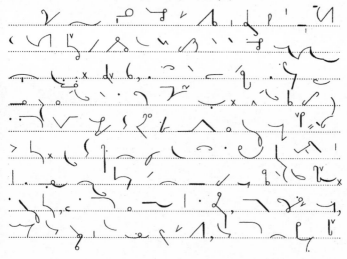

(*Longhand of this passage is on p.* 14)

PASSAGE A (Tape 2—Red Leader)

R.S.A. 80 *words a minute, Summer,* 1967 (I)

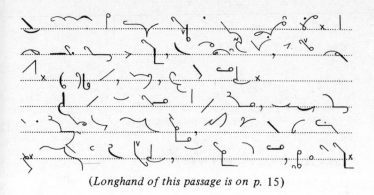

(*Longhand of this passage is on p. 15*)

PASSAGE B (Tape 2—Red Leader)

R.S.A. 80 *words a minute, Summer,* 1967 (II)

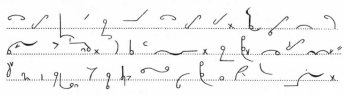

(*Longhand of this passage is on p.* 15)

PASSAGE C (Tape 2—Red Leader)

R.S.A. 80 *words a minute, Summer,* 1967 (III)

(*Longhand of this passage is on p.* 16)

PASSAGE D (Tape 2—Red Leader)

R.S.A. 80 *words a minute, Autumn,* 1967 (I)

(Longhand of this passage is on p. 16)

PASSAGE E (Tape 2—Red Leader)

R.S.A. 80 *words a minute, Autumn,* 1967 (II)

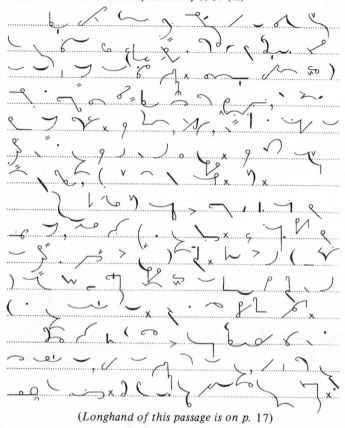

(*Longhand of this passage is on p.* 17)

PASSAGE F (Tape 2—Red Leader)

R.S.A. 80 *words a minute, Autumn,* 1967 (III)

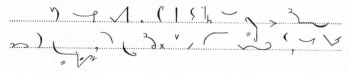

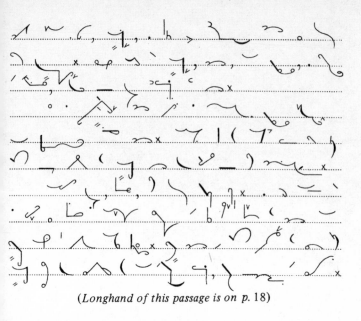

(*Longhand of this passage is on p.* 18)

PASSAGE G (Tape 2—Red Leader)

R.S.A. 80 *words a minute, Easter,* 1968 (I)

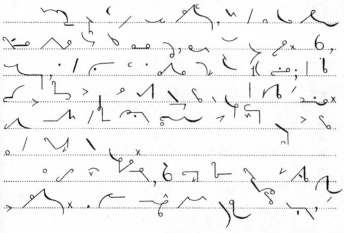

(Longhand of this passage is on p. 18)

PASSAGE H (Tape 2—Red Leader)

R.S.A. 80 words a minute, Easter, 1968 (II)

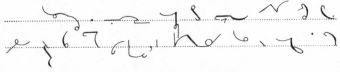

84

(*Longhand of this passage is on p.* 19)

PASSAGE A (Tape 3—White Leader)

R.S.A. 80 words a minute, Whitsun, 1968 (I)

(*Longhand of this passage is on p. 20*)

PASSAGE B (Tape 3—White Leader)

R.S.A. 80 words a minute, Whitsun, 1968 (II)

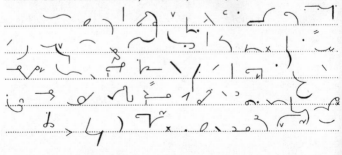

86

(Longhand of this passage is on p. 21)

PASSAGE C (Tape 3—White Leader)

R.S.A. 80 *words a minute, Whitsun,* 1968 (III)

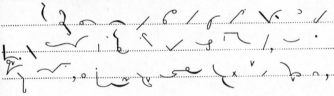

(*Longhand of this passage is on p. 22*)

PASSAGE D (Tape 3—White Leader)

R.S.A. 80 *words a minute, Summer,* 1968 (I)

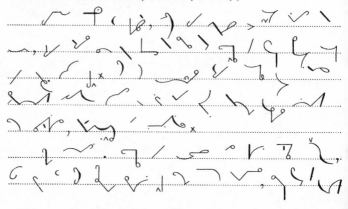

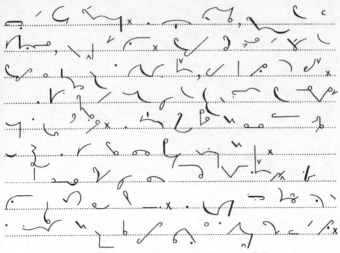

(Longhand of this passage is on p. 22)

PASSAGE E (Tape 3—White Leader)

R.S.A. 80 *words a minute, Summer,* 1968 (II)

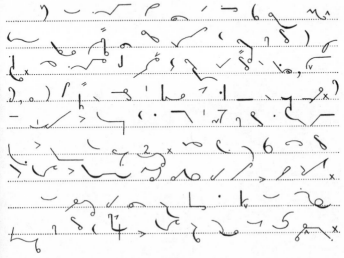

89

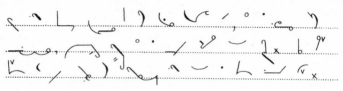

(Longhand of this passage is on p. 23)

PASSAGE F (Tape 3—White Leader)

R.S.A. 80 words a minute, Autumn, 1968 (II)

90

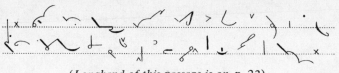

(Longhand of this passage is on p. 23)

PASSAGE G (Tape 3—White Leader)

R.S.A. 80 *words a minute, Whitsun,* 1969 (I)

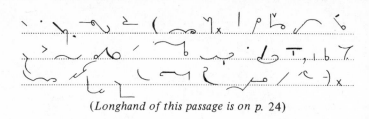

(Longhand of this passage is on p. 24)

PASSAGE H (Tape 3—White Leader)

R.S.A. 80 *words a minute, Whitsun,* 1969 (II)

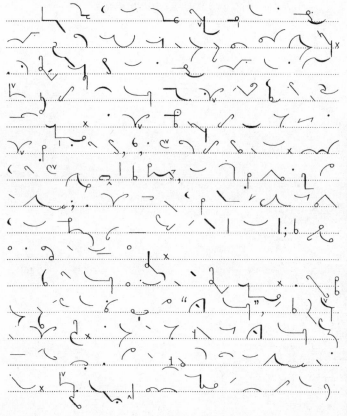

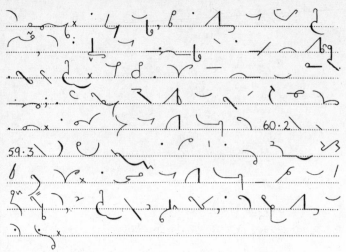

(Longhand of this passage is on p. 25)

PASSAGE A (Tape 3—Red Leader)

R.S.A. 80 *words a minute, Summer,* 1969 (I)

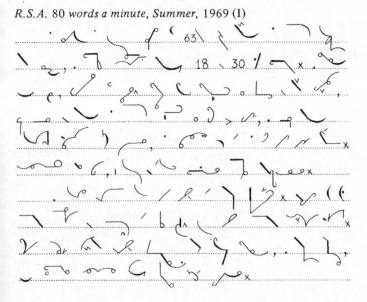

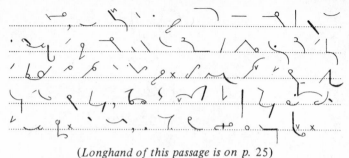

(*Longhand of this passage is on p. 25*)

PASSAGE B (Tape 3–Red Leader)

R.S.A. 80 *words a minute, Summer,* 1969 (II)

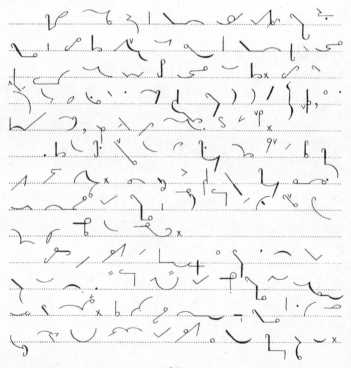

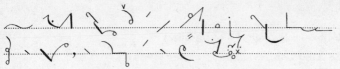

(*Longhand of this passage is on p.* 26)

PASSAGE C (Tape 3—Red Leader)

R.S.A. 80 *words a minute, Summer,* 1969 (III)

(*Longhand of this passage is on p.* 27)

PASSAGE D (Tape 3—Red Leader)

R.S.A 80 *words a minute, Autumn,* 1969 (I)

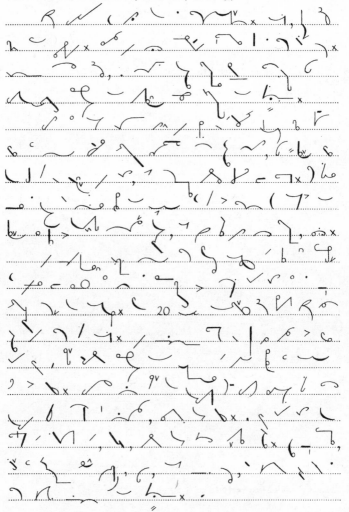

(Longhand of this passage is on p. 27)

PASSAGE E (Tape 3—Red Leader)

R.S.A. 80 *words a minute, Autumn,* 1969 (II)

(*Longhand of this passage is on p.* 28)

PASSAGE F (Tape 3—Red Leader)

R.S.A. 80 *words a minute, Autumn,* 1969 (III)

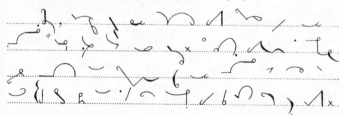

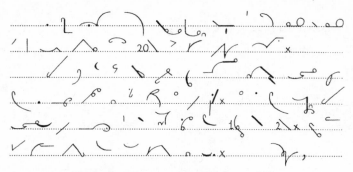

(Longhand of this passage is on p. 29)

PASSAGE G (Tape 3—Red Leader)

Additional Material, 320 *words,* 80 *words a minute*

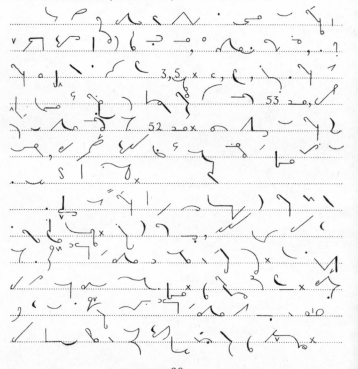

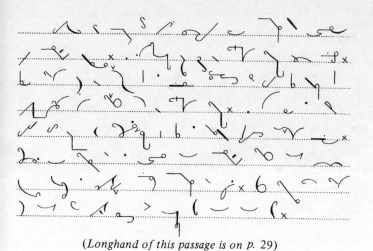

(*Longhand of this passage is on p. 29*)

PASSAGE A (Tape 4—White Leader)

R.S.A. 100 *words a minute, Summer,* 1966 (I)

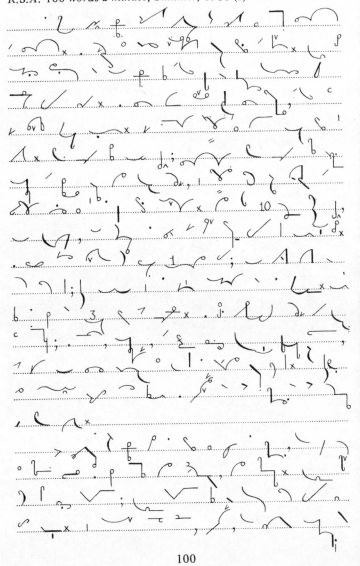

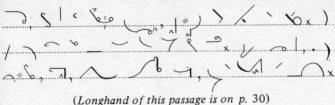

(*Longhand of this passage is on* p. 30)

PASSAGE B (Tape 4—White Leader)

R.S.A. 100 *words a minute, Summer*, 1966 (II)

(Longhand of this passage is on p. 31)

PASSAGE C (Tape 4—White Leader)

R.S.A. 100 *words a minute, Autumn,* 1966 (I)

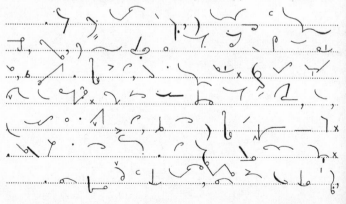

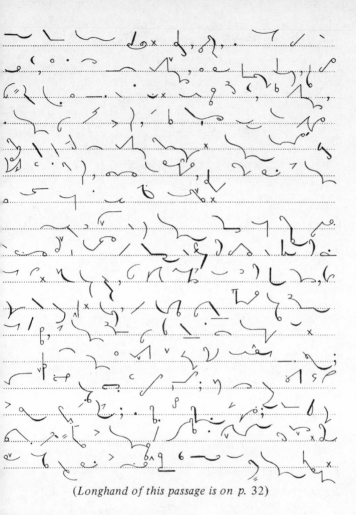

(Longhand of this passage is on p. 32)

PASSAGE D (Tape 4—White Leader)

R.S.A. 100 *words a minute, Autumn,* 1966 (II)

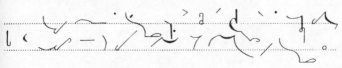

(Longhand of this passage is on p. 33)

PASSAGE E (Tape 4—White Leader)

R.S.A. 100 *words a minute, Autumn,* 1966 (III)

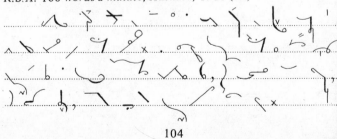

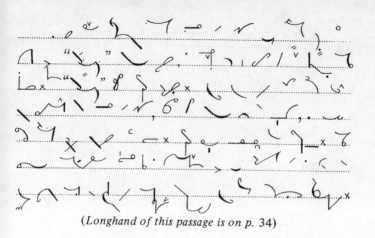

(*Longhand of this passage is on p. 34*)

PASSAGE F (Tape 4—White Leader)

R.S.A. 100 *words a minute, Easter,* 1967 (I)

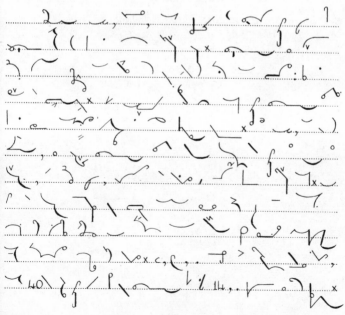

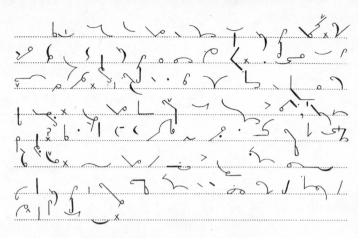

(Longhand of this passage is on p. 34)

PASSAGE G (Tape 4–White Leader)

R.S.A. 100 *words a minute, Easter,* 1967 (II)

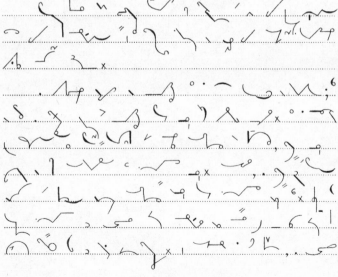

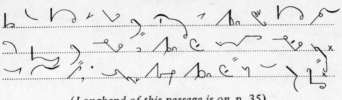

(*Longhand of this passage is on p. 35*)

PASSAGE H (Tape 4—White Leader)

R.S.A. 100 *words a minute, Easter,* 1967 (III)

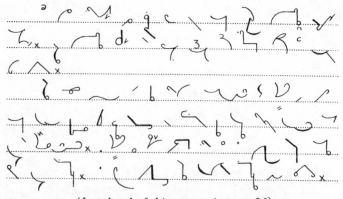

(*Longhand of this passage is on p. 36*)

PASSAGE A (Tape 4—Red Leader)

R.S.A. 100 *words a minute, Whitsun,* 1967 (I)

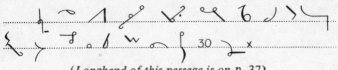

(Longhand of this passage is on p. 37)

PASSAGE B (Tape 4—Red Leader)

R.S.A. 100 *words a minute, Whitsun,* 1967 (II)

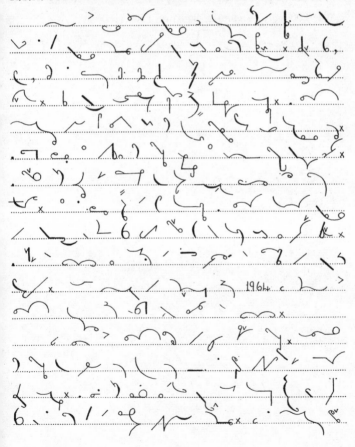

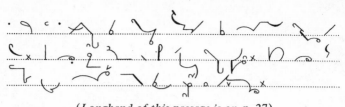

(Longhand of this passage is on p. 37)

PASSAGE C (Tape 4—Red Leader)

R.S.A. 100 *words a minute, Whitsun,* 1967 (III)

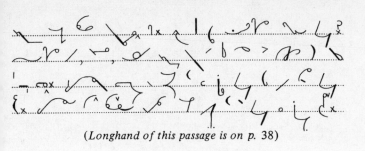

(Longhand of this passage is on p. 38)

PASSAGE D (Tape 4—Red Leader)

R.S.A. 100 *words a minute, Autumn,* 1968 (I)

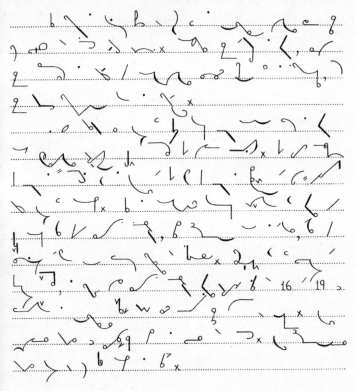

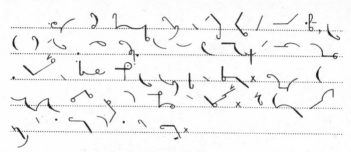

(Longhand of this passage is on p. 39)

PASSAGE E (Tape 4—Red Leader)

R.S.A. 100 *words a minute, Autumn,* 1968 (II)

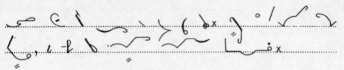

(*Longhand of this passage is on p. 40*)

PASSAGE F (Tape 4—Red Leader)

R.S.A. 100 *words a minute, Autumn,* 1968 (III)

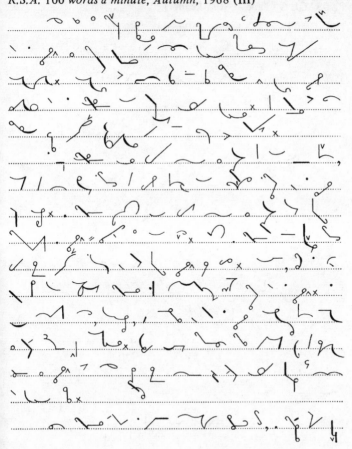

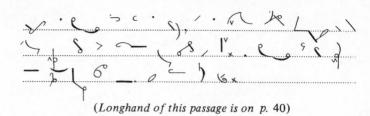

(Longhand of this passage is on p. 40)

PASSAGE G (Tape 4—Red Leader)

R.S.A. 100 *words a minute, Whitsun,* 1969 (I)

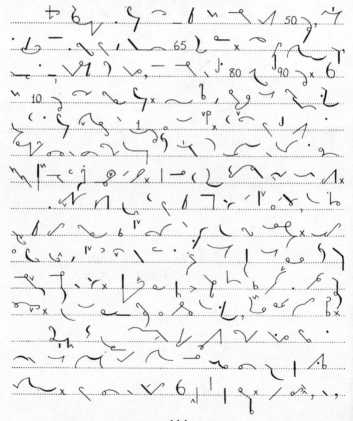

114

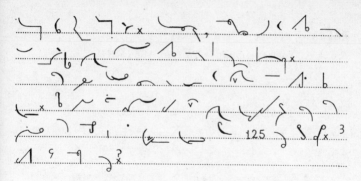

(*Longhand of this passage is on p.* 41)

PASSAGE H (Tape 4—Red Leader)

R.S.A. 100 *words a minute, Whitsun,* 1969 (II)

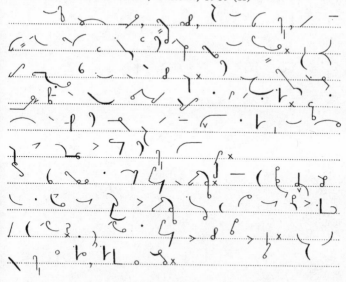

(*Longhand of this passage is on p.* 42)

PASSAGE I (Tape 4—Red Leader)

R.S.A. 100 words a minute, Whitsun, 1969 (III)

(*Longhand of this passage is on p.* 42)

116

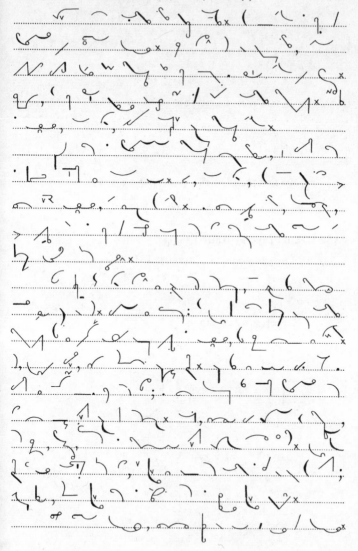

(*Longhand of this passage is on p. 43*)

PASSAGE B (Tape 5—White Leader)

R.S.A. 120 *words a minute, Summer,* 1966 (II)

(*Longhand of this passage is on p.* 44)

PASSAGE C (Tape 5—White Leader)

R.S.A. 120 *words a minute, Autumn,* 1966 (I)

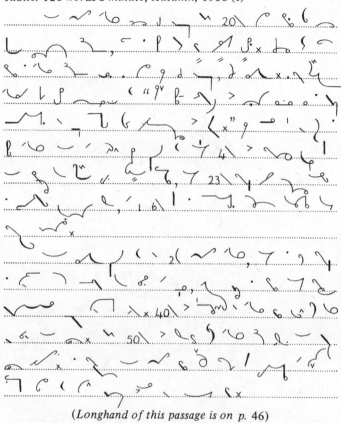

(*Longhand of this passage is on p.* 46)

PASSAGE D (Tape 5—White Leader)

R.S.A. 120 *words a minute, Autumn,* 1966 (II)

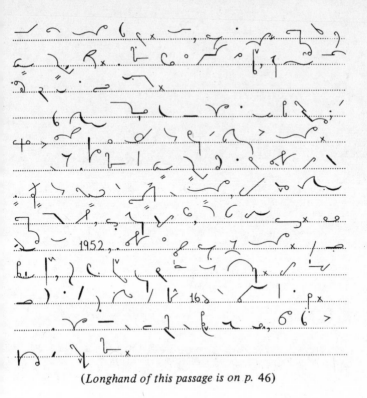

(Longhand of this passage is on p. 46)

PASSAGE E (Tape 5—White Leader)

R.S.A. 120 *words a minute, Summer,* 1968 (II)

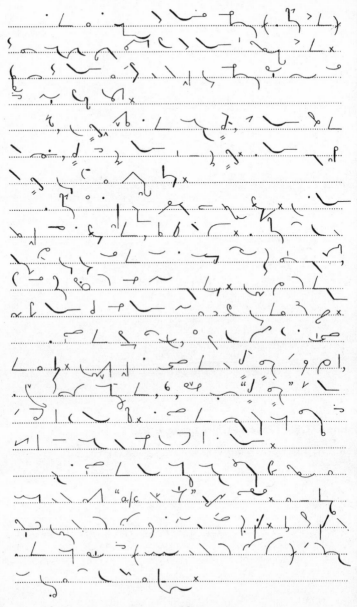

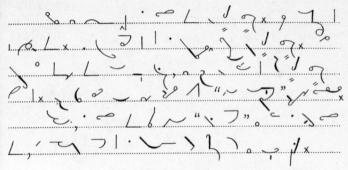

(*Longhand of this passage is on p.* 47)

PASSAGE F (Tape 5—White Leader)

R.S.A. 120 *words a minute, Easter,* 1967 (I)

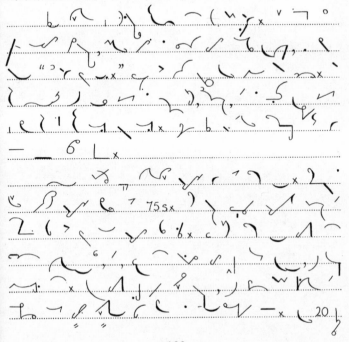

123

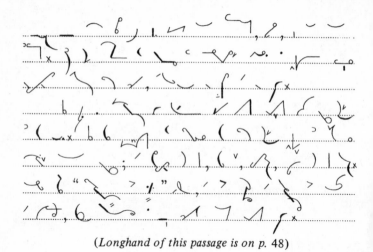

(*Longhand of this passage is on p.* 48)

PASSAGE G (Tape 5–White Leader)

R.S.A. 120 *words a minute, Easter,* 1967 (II)

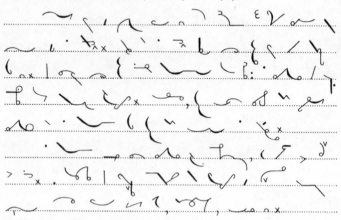

(*Longhand of this passage is on p.* 49)

PASSAGE H (Tape 5–White Leader)

R.S.A. 120 *words a minute, Easter,* 1967 (III)

(Longhand of this passage is on p. 49)

PASSAGE A (Tape 5—Red Leader)

R.S.A. 120 *words a minute, Whitsun,* 1967 (I)

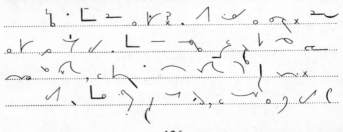

(Longhand of this passage is on p. 51)

PASSAGE B (Tape 5—Red Leader)

R.S.A. 120 *words a minute, Whitsun,* 1967 (II)

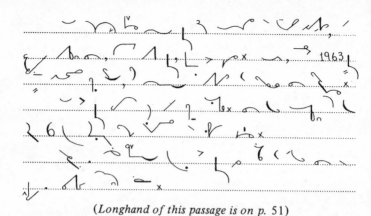

1963

(Longhand of this passage is on p. 51)

PASSAGE C (Tape 5—Red Leader)

R.S.A. 120 *words a minute, Whitsun,* 1967 (III)

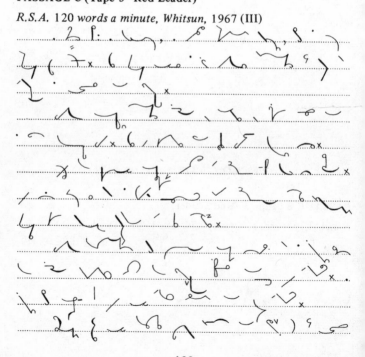

(*Longhand of this passage is on p. 52*)

129

PASSAGE D (Tape 5—Red Leader)

R.S.A. 120 *words a minute, Autumn,* 1967 (I)

(Longhand of this passage is on p. 53)

PASSAGE E (Tape 5—Red Leader)

R.S.A. 120 *words a minute, Autumn,* 1969 (I)

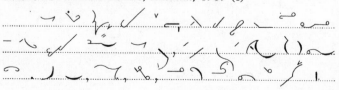

(Longhand of this passage is on p. 54)

PASSAGE F (Tape 5—Red Leader)

R.S.A. 120 *words a minute, Autumn,* 1967 (III)

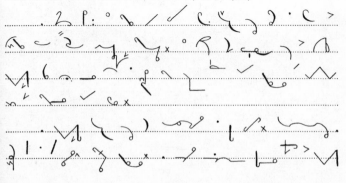

131

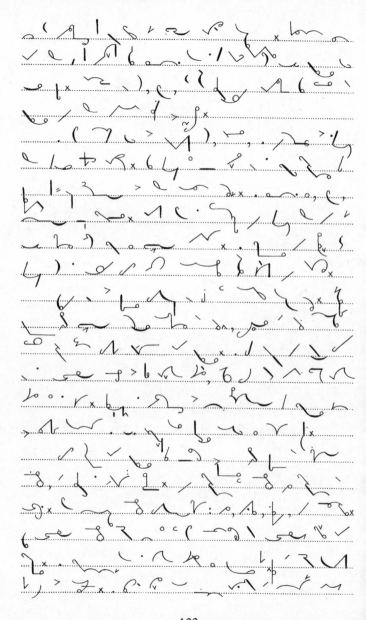

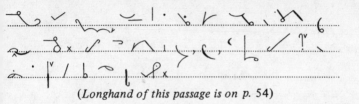

(Longhand of this passage is on p. 54)

PASSAGE G (Tape 5—Red Leader)

R.S.A. 120 *words a minute, Autumn,* 1968 (I)

(*Longhand of this passage is on p. 56*)

PASSAGE H (Tape 5–Red Leader)

R.S.A. 120 *words a minute, Easter,* 1968 (II)

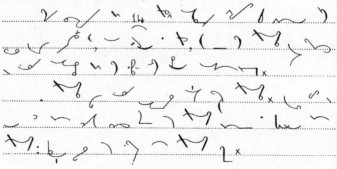

134

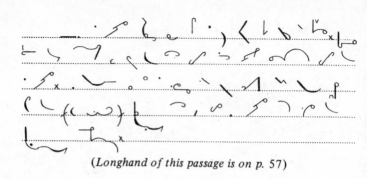

(*Longhand of this passage is on p. 57*)

PAUL MORGAN

Rugby World Cup
2007

PaRragon

Bath • New York • Singapore • Hong Kong • Cologne • Delhi • Melbourne

C O N T

introduction 4

PART ONE
let battle commence 10

POOL A 12
England 12   South Africa 18   USA 22
Samoa 24   Tonga 25   Pool A Stadium 26

POOL B 28
Australia 28   Wales 34   Fiji 38
Canada 40   Japan 41   Pool B Stadium 42

POOL C 44
New Zealand 44   Scotland 50   Italy 54
Romania 56   Portugal 57   Pool C
Stadium 58

POOL D 60
France 60   Ireland 66   Argentina 70
Namibia 72   Georgia 73   Pool D
Stadium 74

PART TWO
heroes in waiting 76

Marco Bortolami Italy 78
Dan Carter New Zealand 79
Rupeni Caucaunibuca Fiji 80
Fourie Du Preez South Africa 82
Gavin Henson Wales 83
Yannick Jauzion France 84
Chris Latham Australia 85
Josh Lewsey England 86
Brian Lima Samoa 88
Richie McCaw New Zealand 90
Yannick Nyanga France 92
Paul O'Connell Ireland 93
Brian O'Driscoll Ireland 94
Daisuke Ohata Japan 95
Gareth Thomas Wales 96
Jason White Scotland 98

E N T S

PART THREE
the path to glory 100

1987 **NEW ZEALAND** 102
1991 **AUSTRALIA** 106
1995 **SOUTH AFRICA** 109
1999 **AUSTRALIA** 112
2003 **ENGLAND** 116

PART FOUR
inside the game 120

WORLD CUP RECORDS 121
THE MEN IN THE MIDDLE 122
THE INSIDE TRACK 124
PICTURE CREDITS 128

the webb ellis cup

THE GAME TOOK SHAPE
AT RUGBY SCHOOL IN
WARWICKSHIRE, THE
SPIRITUAL HOME OF
RUGBY UNION

Rugby, like many sports, evolved over the centuries and has its heritage in the ball games that were played through the 18th and early 19th centuries. The game of rugby union almost certainly did not kick off for the first time with a young man called William Webb Ellis picking up the ball and running with it. That incredible story – which only surfaced after his death in 1872 – is best regarded as apocryphal, but Webb Ellis and his contemporaries at Rugby School were crucial in the establishment of the sport.

Historians believe that rugby developed out of one of the many sports, such as Camp-Ball and the Eton Wall game, played at England's public schools and, in particular, Rugby School in the early to mid-19th century. There are stories of senior boys at Rugby School meeting in the evening to review the games and suggest amendments for the following day's contests. The first set of rules – which would be unrecognisable from today's rugby union – surfaced around 1845 and it was these that those senior boys adjusted.

Jonny Wilkinson must be delighted he was not around at that time, as those early rules sound crazy today. They included the tactic of hacking, which allowed one player to kick another in the shins. The 2003 World Cup Final might have had a completely different ending had the Wallabies been able to kick Wilkinson in the shins! "Hacking was permitted in those rules," reported *The Daily Telegraph* in 1846, "but not above the knee. Holding a player, carrying the ball is permitted but with one arm only. Running in is permitted but passing with the hands is banned. And if no decision is reached after five afternoons of play, a match will be declared drawn."

story

Two major splits defined the sport we see today. The first came in 1863 when rugby football broke away from the Football Association to form its own game. The Rugby Association wanted to pick up the ball and run with it while they insisted on keeping their affinity with "hacking". Both of these principles were against the essence of football and so the first split was set.

Test match rugby makes its debut

The first rugby union international was staged in 1871 between Scotland and England, in Edinburgh, and won by the Scots in front of around 4,000 spectators – a few thousand less than the Calcutta Cup match would attract today! The teams for this first international were 20-a-side, the test match lasting two periods of 50 minutes, 20 minutes longer than in the modern game. In 1871 another momentous day occurred when the first senior club – Neath RFC – was formed in Wales, and a year later British residents at Le Havre established the first French team.

The formation of the International Rugby Board, where the rules of the game would be enshrined, then followed. The game was very much the preserve of the home nations (England, Scotland, Ireland and Wales) and then in 1895 came rugby's greatest split, when rugby divided into league and union. The greybeards met in Huddersfield and 20 clubs from Cheshire, Lancashire and Yorkshire decided to go their own way and form a new game called rugby league.

The crucial division came about because of money. In rugby league players would be paid to play the new game and the teams would only consist of 13-a-side. Players in working-class areas found it tough to continue playing an amateur game. Unlike some of their richer counterparts in the south, they found it more difficult to play just for the love of the game and what would happen if injury struck? Many of the clubs in the south were made up of ex-public school boys, so the players were in a better position – financially –

to enshrine the principles of an amateur sport.

France's early love of rugby led to the sport being involved in the Olympics, where the father of the Games, Pierre de Coubertin, made sure it was part of the family. France won the first gold, at the Paris Games in 1900, and although it was again played in 1908 and 1920 it was cut from the list of sports in 1924 with the USA winning the last gold medal, in Paris.

While the divisions were occurring in England – around the turn of the 20th century – the game of rugby union was spreading to countries across the world, most notably to New Zealand and South Africa, where it received an enthusiastic response. Former Rugby schoolboys can be thanked for helping develop the game in many

HARROW SCHOOL WAS ONE OF THE ENGLISH PUBLIC SCHOOLS SO IMPORTANT IN THE DEVELOPMENT OF THE GAME OF RUGBY UNION

countries as they travelled in the decades after its establishment.

A Home International Championship was first started in 1883, with England as the inaugural winners, in the same year that Ned Haig, the Melrose butcher, devised the truncated version of rugby – sevens. To win that first Championship England claimed victories over Wales, Scotland and Ireland, the Scottish win being England's first triumph north of the border. In 1910 the four became five, when France was admitted to the Championship, welcomed with a 49–14 hammering by Wales. France had to wait until their second Championship – in 1911 – to record their first win. However, it was a controversial kick-off for the French: in 1914 Scotland refused to travel to Paris after allegations that the Scottish players and the English referee were mobbed and assaulted at the end of the previous game in the French capital. Almost 90 years later, in 2000, Italy turned the Five Nations into Six; after the 2006 Championship England still led the way with 25 outright wins.

On the road to the Rugby World Cup

With football starting its own World Cup in 1930, it was inevitable that one day rugby would have their own world championship. As the decades went on the series between New Zealand and South Africa decided the title of unofficial world champion, and between them they totally dominated the rugby world. Scotland and Ireland still have not recorded a single win over New Zealand, while Wales have to go back as far as 1953 to remember their last victory against the All Blacks. It was not until 2003 that England managed to beat both New Zealand and Australia on their own soil in a 12-month period. England's 15–13 victory in Wellington was their first in New Zealand since 1973.

Either side of World War II no-one came close to threatening the domination of New Zealand and South Africa, and even into the 1960s the two sides rarely suffered defeats outside of games against each other. Australia, a country dominated by rugby league, is an infant in rugby union terms, not making a big impact on the world stage until the 1984 tourists completed a Grand Slam while on a European tour, beating England, Wales, Scotland and Ireland.

The New Zealanders, in contrast, toured Europe in 1905 under captain Dave Gallaher. They were first christened The Originals and when they arrived again – in 1924 – the moniker had changed to The Invincibles. The Originals set high standards for teams arriving in Europe from New Zealand, scoring an average of 28 points a game and keeping the opposition scoreless in 23 of their 35 games. The boys at Rugby School may have given birth to the game but The Invincibles defined so many parts of the game we see today. Captained by Cliff Porter, and including the peerless full-back George Nepia, this New Zealand side stayed in Europe for six months winning all 32 of their games – which included four test matches – scoring 838 points and only conceding 116. Nepia played in every game.

The term All Blacks – to describe the New Zealand team – was first used during the 1905 tour when the All Blacks lost 3–0 to Wales, but the true origins of the name are still not known. This was the first side to leave New Zealand for Europe and a report in the *Daily Mail* referred to them as "All Blacks", coining one of the most famous nicknames in the

THE 1905 ORIGINALS TOURING TEAM FROM NEW ZEALAND SHAPED RUGBY UNION IN THE EARLY 20TH CENTURY AND SET NEW STANDARDS FOR THE SIDES IN EUROPE. (BELOW) THEIR FIXTURE LIST SHOWS HOW ARDUOUS THEIR TRIP TO EUROPE WAS

rugby world. In 1905 the first sightings of a haka were also made. The first rugby match on the New Zealand islands took place between Nelson College and Nelson football club in 1870. "Credit for the introduction of rugby to New Zealand goes to Charles John Monro, son of Sir David Monro, Speaker in the House of Representatives from 1860 to 1870," according to the New Zealand Rugby Football Union. "Charles Monro, who was born at Waimea East, was sent to Christ's College, Finchley in England to complete his education and while there he learned the rugby game. On his return to Nelson he suggested that the

FIXTURES.

Date.	Opponent.	Ground.	Result.
Sept. 16	Devon	Exeter	55pt. to 4
„ 20	Cornwall	Redruth	41 „ 0
„ 23	Bristol	Bristol	41 „ 0
„ 28	Northampton	Northampton	32 „ 0
„ 30	Leicester	Leicester	28 „ 0
Oct. 4	Middlesex	London	34 „ 0
„ 7	Durham		16 „ 3
„ 11	The Hartlepools	Hartlepool	63 „ 0
„ 14	Northumberland	North Shields	31 „ 0
„ 19	Gloucester City	Gloucester	44 „ 0
„ 21	Somerset	Taunton	23 „ 0
„ 25	Devonport Albion	Devonport	21 „ 3
„ 28	Midland Counties	Leicester	21 „ 5
Nov. 1	Surrey	Richmond	11 „ 0
„ 4	Blackheath	Blackheath	
„ 7	Oxford Univers'y	Oxford	
„ 9	Cambridge „	Cambridge	
„ 11	Richmond	Richmond	
„ 15	Bedford	Bedford	
„ 18	Scotland	Edinburgh	
„ 22	West of Scotland	Glasgow	
„ 25	Ireland	Dublin	
„ 29	Munster	Limerick	
Dec. 2	England	Crystal Palace	
„ 6	Cheltenham	Cheltenham	
„ 9	Cheshire	Birkenhead	
„ 13	Yorkshire		
„ 16	Wales	Cardiff	
„ 23	Newport	Newport	
„ 26	Cardiff	Cardiff	
„ 30	Swansea	Swansea	
		Total Points up to date 461	15

AGES, WEIGHTS, & HEIGHTS.

BACKS.
	Age, st. lbs. ft. in.
W. Wallace	27 .. 12 0 .. 5 8
E. Harper	27 .. 12 7 .. 5 11
E. Booth	26 .. 11 10 .. 5 7½
G. W. Smith	33 .. 11 12 .. 5 7
H. Abbott	22 .. 13 0 .. 5 10½
F. Roberts	21 .. 13 4 .. 6 0
J. Hunter	26 .. 11 8 .. 5 7
S. Mynott	29 .. 11 0 .. 5 6
G. Gillett	28 .. 13 0 .. 6 0
R. McGregor	24 .. 16 9 .. 5 8
H. D. Thomson	23 .. 11 9 .. 5 5
Manager—MR. DIXON.	

FORWARDS.
	Age, st. lbs. ft. in.
D. Gallaher (Capt.)	29 .. 13 0 .. 6 0
W. S. Glenn	27 .. 12 12 .. 5 11
S. Casey	22 .. 12 13 .. 5 10
A. McDonald	22 .. 13 6 .. 5 10
W. Johnstone	23 .. 13 0 .. 6 0
C. Seeling	22 .. 13 7 .. 6 0
G. Nicholson	26 .. 13 10 .. 6 0
G. A. Tyler	25 .. 13 5 .. 5 11
J. Corbett	25 .. 13 0 .. 6 0
F. Newton	22 .. 13 6 .. 5 10
F. Glasgow	25 .. 12 7 .. 5 10
J. O'Sullivan	22 .. 13 7 .. 5 11
W. Mackrell	23 .. 11 3 .. 5 6
W. Cunningham	29 .. 14 6 .. 5 11

local football club try out the rugby rules. The game must have appealed to the club members for they decided to adopt it."

Following the split from rugby league in 1896, rugby waited almost 100 years for its next big step, into the world of professional sport. Staunchly amateur for those 100 years to such an extent that players were banned for life just for being paid to write a book or for daring to even have a trial with a rugby league side, the game went professional overnight. In August 1995 the International Rugby Board declared rugby union "open" after a meeting of the major test playing unions. What became clear at that meeting was that long before the game became professional in 1995, the majority of countries were already paying their players, without sanction.

It was vital that the IRB acted in 1995 because if they had done nothing the world's leading players would have almost certainly been signed to an alternative tournament, funded by big business. "The changes are a reflection of the way the game has changed since the seventies when players were not only unpaid but banned from making money even indirectly from the game – for example writing their memoirs or for newspapers," it was reported in *The Daily Telegraph*. "By the early eighties under the counter payments such as 'boot money' from kit manufacturers and inflated expenses became increasingly common."

The Lions make their presence known

Throughout rugby's history the only way the nations of England, Scotland, Ireland and Wales could consistently challenge the giants of New Zealand or South Africa was through the formation of the world famous British and Irish Lions, who did much to promote the game in all corners of the earth. The Lions – a touring side made up of the best players from England, Scotland, Ireland and Wales – first toured in 1888 and have enjoyed a rich history ever since. Early tours were largely Anglo-Welsh affairs, but in 1910 players from all four nations headed to South Africa – under Dr Tom Smythe – losing the test series 2–1.

Many feared that professionalism would see an end to the Lions, but they have gone from strength to strength since the mid-1990s. The venerable *Times* writer John Hopkins summed up brilliantly what a Lions' tour is when he said: "A major rugby tour by the British Isles to New Zealand is a cross between a medieval

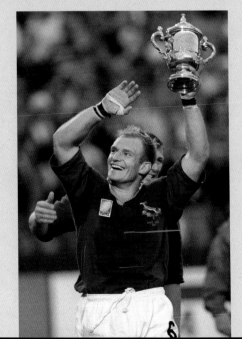

INTRODUCTION

crusade and a prep school outing." The Lions triumphed in their first professional tour in 1997 – under the captaincy of Martin Johnson they won the series 2–1. That victory was not repeated in 2001 when they made the trip to Australia, and when they left New Zealand in 2005 they had suffered the greatest hammering in their history. But those three tours ensured the Lions were here to stay. "The Lions is different in the professional age; it is almost a romantic team rather than a built-up team," said Sir Clive Woodward, who coached the Lions in 2005. He went on, "The Lions are very special. I still think the Lions is a great concept. The supporters over there were just fantastic, they have all had a great trip and hopefully they will do so again in South Africa in four years' time." In 2005 the Lions were followed by 20,000 fans from the UK and Ireland.

JONNY WILKINSON DELIVERED THE WORLD CUP TO ENGLAND FOR THE FIRST TIME IN 2003, KICKING A LAST-MINUTE DROP GOAL AS THEY WON 20–17 AGAINST AUSTRALIA

Calls for a Rugby World Cup first surfaced in the 1970s but were rebuffed as the major nations feared that with a World Cup would come professionalism. Of course they were right. But in the end those members of the old guard who protected amateurism – and opposed a World Cup – were washed over like King Canute, and it is significant that the game went professional just after the 1995 World Cup was held in South Africa. Australia and New Zealand were the key movers in the establishment of a World Cup, and were therefore the obvious choices as joint hosts when it first kicked off in 1987.

Each subsequent World Cup has been bigger than the one before with the 2003 tournament – won by England – breaking a number of records. Just under 2 million spectators watched the 48 games in 2003, with a worldwide television audience of 3.5 billion from 205 countries. The web site www.rugbyworldcup.com had 495 million hits during the tournament, including 44.5 million hits on the day of the Final. The Final itself attracted the largest ever World Cup crowd – 82,957. "Australia has put on the best ever World Cup, Australia has again done itself proud on the world stage," said Australian Rugby Union Chief Executive John O'Neill, "The atmosphere was extraordinary. Being at the match venues you had to do a double take. At times you read the newspapers and you wondered if there was anything else going on in the world. When people talk about reliving the Olympic spirit (Sydney Olympics) they will talk about reliving the Olympic spirit and the Rugby World Cup spirit." That spirit has remained since 2003 and shows no indication of waning.

THE HISTORY OF POINTS SCORING Rugby union's points system has evolved since the first one was established in 1890. The changes were:

DATE	TRY	PENALTY
1890–91	1 Point	2 Points
1891–92	2 Points	3 Points
1893–94	3 Points	3 Points
1971–72	4 Points	3 Points
1992–93	5 Points	3 Points

let battle com

mence O N E

POOL A

POOL B

POOL C

POOL D

POOL A England

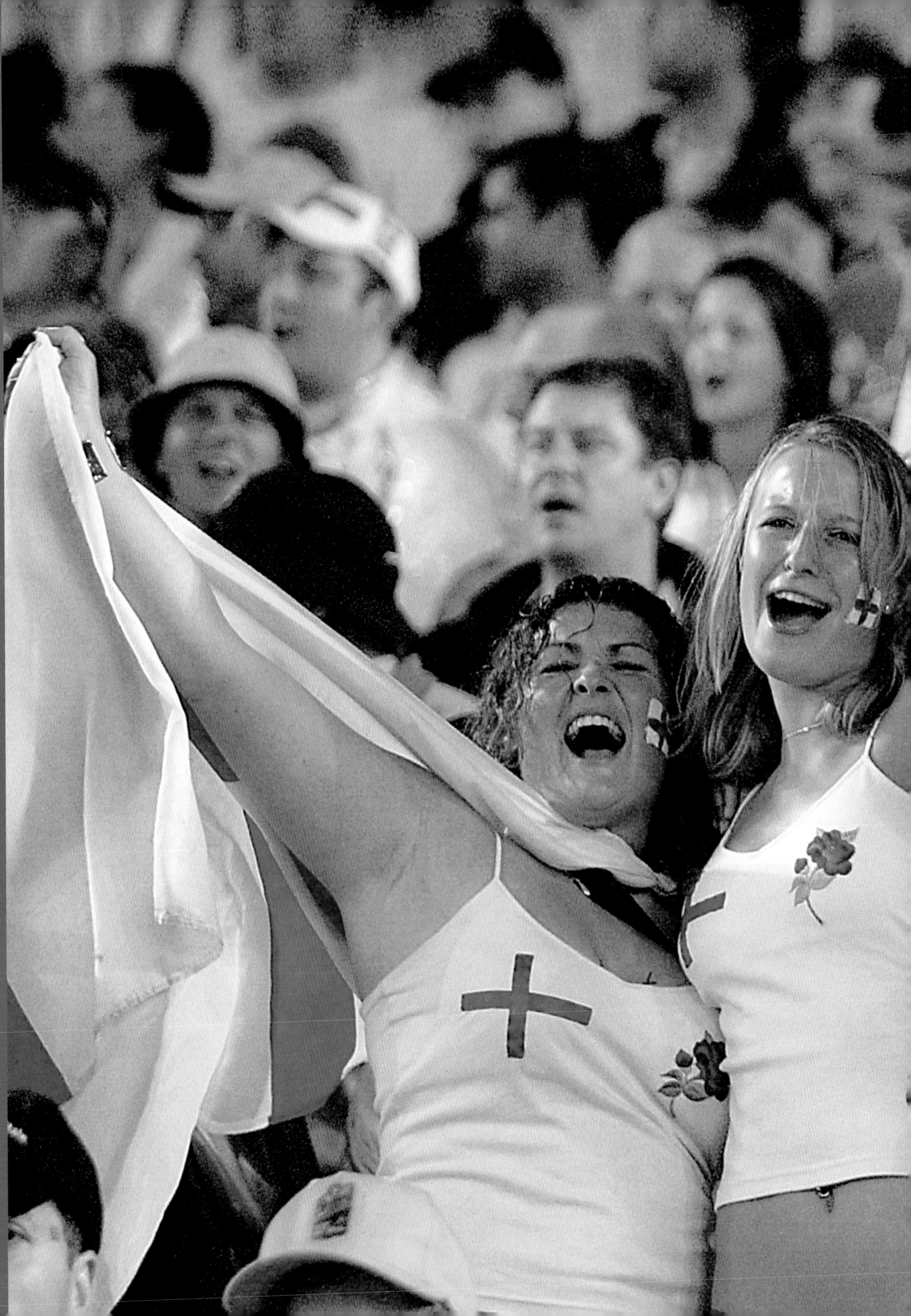

Can England double it up?

When Martin Johnson (left) lifted the Webb Ellis Cup in 2003, England became the first side from the northern hemisphere to become world champions. Win it again in 2007 and they would make history as the first side to retain rugby's greatest prize.

In 2007 the holders have been drawn in a group almost exactly the same as the one they overcame four years ago, with the seminal match against South Africa. This time though the game will take place in the 80,000-seater Stade de France, rather than in Perth.

One thing that is for certain is that the England that turns up in 2007 will be radically different from the one that held the World Cup aloft at Sydney's Telstra Stadium on 22 November 2003.

Gone are coach Sir Clive Woodward, captain Martin Johnson and a host of other players including Jason Leonard, Trevor Woodman, Neil Back, Matt Dawson and Will Greenwood.

Without these guiding lights and because of a series of long-term injuries to their hero in 2003 – Jonny Wilkinson – England have endured a rough ride as world champions, and will not go into the 2007 tournament as one of the favourites.

Fourth in the Six Nations Championship in 2004, 2005 and 2006 is unacceptable for an England team that was also humiliated by a seven-match losing run in 2006, a year when they only beat Italy, Wales and South Africa.

ENGLAND AND JOSH LEWSEY (ABOVE) WERE
SHACKLED BY SCOTLAND IN 2006 (ABOVE) WHILE
TRIES HAVE BECOME A PRECIOUS COMMODITY
SINCE 2003 – MARK CUETO GOING OVER FOR ONE
AGAINST ITALY (RIGHT)

England 0 Wales 0

But the real indication of how far England had fallen came in November 2006 when Argentina claimed their first-ever victory at Twickenham, and England were left seventh in the world rankings, the lowest position in their history.

This run culminated in Andy Robinson – the coach who replaced Woodward – leaving his post 10 months before the start of the World Cup.

"We've got from first to sixth in the world in 18 months and those rankings do reflect your standing," said former England Captain Fran Cotton, who supports central contracts to help the future of English rugby.

"I think the best idea is for England to select the 100 players they want in the squad, to sign them on and to pay them. The clubs will sign the players that they want to play and we'll go about it that way. There's plenty of other Jonny Wilkinsons coming behind."

ENGLAND KICKED OFF 2006 IN FINE STYLE (LEFT) BEATING WALES 47–13, AND EVEN FOLLOWED THAT UP WITH A 31–16 VICTORY OVER ITALY (ABOVE) BUT AFTER THAT THEY SUCCUMBED TO SEVEN SUCCESSIVE DEFEATS

Springboks hope for a new start

When the draw for the World Cup was made in 2004 South Africa could hardly believe their bad luck, drawn in the same group as the holders – England – and the dangerous Samoans. But by 2006 that draw was looking kind to Jake White's South Africa, when they completed a miserable year for England by winning 25–14 at Twickenham. The victory – at the home of English rugby – ended a shocking run of seven successive defeats for South Africa at Twickenham. "Today was a massive win, a huge step forward," said South Africa coach Jake White. "Winning at Twickenham for the first time since 1997 is a huge psychological boost. The big thing of course is the World Cup. Beating the world champions at home 10 months before the World Cup is huge."

White took the calculated gamble of leaving 10 of his best players at home – to rest – before making the trip to Europe to take on not only England but Ireland as well.

SOUTH AFRICA WERE THE ONLY SIDE TO INFLICT DEFEAT ON THE RAMPANT NEW ZEALAND ALL BLACKS IN 2006, SKIPPERED BY JOHN SMIT (RIGHT, BELOW)

MARIUS JOUBERT, ONE OF A GROUP OF EXCITING
YOUNG SPRINGBOKS BACKS WHO HAVE THE ABILITY
TO LIGHT UP THE 2007 WORLD CUP

However it was a gamble that paid off handsomely, not only with the victory at Twickenham but with the discovery of a new generation of Springboks, who are set to light up the 2007 World Cup. Players like François Steyn, Kabamba Floors and Chiliboy Ralepelle were virtual unknowns outside South Africa before the 2006 tour but showed their brilliance, ensuring that White will have a tough selection dilemma in 2007. Ralepelle was handed a further honour at the end of the tour, captaining the side against a World XV, the first black player to skipper South Africa in a major international match.

SOUTH AFRICA'S COACH JAKE
WHITE (ABOVE) SURVIVED CALLS
FOR HIS RESIGNATION IN
2006...HIS SIDE HAS ONE OF THE
WORLD'S BEST LINEOUT
EXPONENTS IN VICTOR MATFIELD
(RIGHT, IN GREEN)

POOL A – SOUTH AFRICA

USA Eagles face a mountain to climb

The USA Eagles became the 13th side to qualify for the World Cup, winning an Americas play-off against Uruguay in October 2006. They secured a 75–20 aggregate victory over the Uruguayans to move into pool one. Having been defeated in record fashion by arch rivals Canada in the Americas Two decider, USA entered their two-match play-off series with a lot to prove. "I was very pleased with the end result," USA Rugby's Interim Head Coach Peter Thorburn said. "Our goal was to qualify for the Rugby World Cup, and we are delighted to have achieved that goal. We can now focus on preparing for the tournament next year and the exciting challenge of facing reigning champions England in our opening match." The USA have only won two games, despite making four of the five World Cup finals, both against Japan, in 1987 and 2003.

USA (ABOVE) CELEBRATE THEIR WIN OVER JAPAN IN 2003 WHILE DAVE HODGES (LEFT) WINS SOME LINEOUT BALL AGAINST FRANCE

Beware the rugby warriors of Samoa

Back in 1991 Western Samoa – as they were called then – caused the first and perhaps the biggest upset in Rugby World Cup history, beating Wales 16–13 in Cardiff. This time around – in 2007 – they are faced with a similar task, after being drawn, for the second successive tournament, with holders England, and former winners South Africa.

Michael Jones' Samoans ran through their qualification with ease, beating Fiji and Tonga to take their place in their fifth successive Rugby World Cup finals. Asserting their supremacy in the Pacific Islands, they scored 50 points against Tonga and 36 against Fiji.

STEPHEN SO'OIALO
(RIGHT) BRINGS THE
EXPERIENCE OF THE
GUINNESS PREMIERSHIP
TO THE SAMOA SIDE

Off to France, in style

Tonga scored an impressive 13 tries to qualify for the World Cup and take their place alongside England, South Africa, Samoa and USA in Pool A, with a win over Korea. Hudson Tonga'uiha, Fangatapu Apikotoa and wingers Vaea Poteki and Sione Fonua all scored twice as the South Sea Islanders confirmed their spot in France.

TONGA COMPLETE POOL A, AFTER THEIR 83–3 QUALIFICATION VICTORY OVER KOREA, IN AUCKLAND

POOL A

Tonga

Fit for a king

The 80,000 capacity Stade de France is the centrepiece of the 2007 Rugby World Cup and will house the crucial Pool A game between England and South Africa on 14 September. Opened in 1998 for the Football World Cup, it earned a special place in the heart of the French nation as it staged the subsequent final and France's 3–0 win over Brazil.

THE COLOUR AND PAGEANTRY OF THE STADE DE FRANCE – ONE OF THE WORLD'S GREATEST STADIUMS – WILL ENSURE AN UNFORGETTABLE RUGBY WORLD CUP

Australia are flying

When Australia lifted the Webb Ellis Cup for a second time in 1999, they won a tournament based in the northern hemisphere. The same was the case eight years earlier when they were victorious for the first time. An omen perhaps for the 2007 campaign as the Wallabies are facing the same conditions this time around.

Back in 1999, the Wallabies were one of the World Cup favourites, but a shocking 2005, when they lost seven consecutive Tests will ensure that they are not one of the fancied teams this time round. That destruction of their reputation was due, in part, to the way their forward pack had been dismantled by some of the other top nations. No one has ever had anything but the highest respect for

their backline, which is set to arrive in Wales as one of the most highly regarded in the world.

And of course the Wallabies have the Gregan factor. George Gregan will come into the 2007 World Cup as the most-capped player in the history of the game, having passed Jason Leonard's previous high mark in the summer of 2006.

Gregan was rested for the November 2006 tour of Europe so he could be in peak condition when it is time for the trophies to be handed out in France.

John Connolly – appointed Australia coach in 2006 – has set his sights on developing his pack but a 29–29 draw

NATHAN SHARPE (BELOW LEFT) IS THE HEARTBEAT OF AN AUSTRALIAN PACK THAT NEEDS TO STEP UP TO THE PLATE IN 2007, WHILE THE BACKLINE, WHICH INCLUDES DREW MITCHELL (BELOW RIGHT), HAS THE ABILITY TO TROUBLE ANY SIDE IN THE WORLD

THE WALLABIES WILL BE
CHEERED ON BY LEGIONS OF
FANS IN FRANCE (LEFT) WHILE
THEY WILL BE LOOKING FOR
TRIES LIKE THIS FROM MARK
CHISHOLM (BELOW) AGAINST
ITALY IN 2005

with Wales and a comprehensive defeat to Ireland, a year from the finals will have done a great deal of damage to his ambitions.

At least the Wallabies ended their November 2006 European tour with a victory, beating Scotland 44–15. This was a huge improvement on 2005, when they lost seven consecutive games, an awful run that cost former Australia coach Eddie Jones his job.

"You're not going to go from losing a lot on the trot to winning every game overnight," said Connolly, who

confirmed that unlike the New Zealand All Blacks, his
Wallaby players would not be afforded a rest during the
2007 Super 14 campaign.

"We're happy with the forwards' progress but with
the backs we've got a few steps to go."

Time for Wales to impress

Wales have a World Cup record that bears no resemblance to their place in rugby's history and they have underachieved in almost every one of the five finals.

One of the fabled sides of rugby, their halcyon days of the 1970s – when they ruled the world – came long before the advent of a Rugby World Cup.

After finishing a creditable third in 1987, they proceeded to lose to Samoa in both 1991 and 1999, while suffering at the hands of the New Zealand All Blacks in South Africa in 1995.

But this time round they have been handed a golden chance to make it through beyond the quarter-finals after organisers announced some games would be staged in Wales.

Wales have the distinct advantage of playing their key pool match – against Australia – at their very own Millennium Stadium, where the Wallabies haven't won since 2001.

The last game between the sides in Cardiff – in 2006 –

WALES WILL NEED FLYERS LIKE SHANE WILLIAMS (BELOW) ON TOP FORM IF THEY ARE TO TOPPLE THE WALLABIES AS THEY DID IN 2005 (RIGHT)

was a stunning 29–29 draw, sealed by a late penalty from fly-half James Hook.

The added edge to the game sees former Wales coach, Scott Johnson, as now the attack specialist for Australia.

"The one that really counts is the World Cup," said Wales captain Gareth Thomas. "We are improving and so are they, so hopefully it will be a classic."

Wales finished off 2006 with a 45–10 defeat to New Zealand in Cardiff.

"New Zealand are, at the present time, probably better than anyone else in every department," admitted Wales coach Gareth Jenkins.

SHANE WILLIAMS SKIPS AWAY
FROM LOTE TUQIRI DURING
WALES' 24–22 VICTORY IN 2005

GAVIN HENSON (ABOVE) IS
SET TO BE ONE OF THE HIGH
PROFILE PLAYERS AT THE
WORLD CUP WHILE GARETH
THOMAS (LEFT) WILL BE
PLAYING IN HIS FOURTH,
AND ALMOST CERTAINLY
LAST, FINALS

Ready to fulfill their destiny

Fiji are masters of the Sevens game but have yet to make the breakthrough in the 15-a-side code that their skills richly deserve.

Quarter-finalists in 1995, they will be dangerous outsiders in 2007, especially if their pack can get much-needed balls for their devastating backline.

This time round they will need to target the games against Wales and Australia, and they have been helped with the draw as they are playing Wales in Nantes, rather than Cardiff.

One thing that is for sure is that they have one of the most explosive players at the tournament with wing Rupeni Caucaunibuca, who is playing in his second World Cup.

Caucau, as he is better known, came so close to sending Fiji into the last eight in 2003, scoring two tries in the crucial game against Scotland, only to see the Scots snatch a 22–20 victory in the closing minutes.

"He could be a superstar," said Fiji's coach at the 2003 World Cup Mac McCallion. "He's got a great future – he's probably got more potential than any other player that I've been involved with or seen."

API NAEVO (TOP), ALFRED ULUINAYAU (ABOVE) AND VILIMONI DELASAU (RIGHT) DID MUCH TO KEEP THE FIJIAN FANS HAPPY IN 2003, JUST FAILING – BY TWO POINTS – TO MAKE THE QUARTER-FINALS OF THE WORLD CUP

Canucks hope to turn the tables

When Canada lost to Wales in 2006 at the Millennium Stadium, Canada coach Ric Suggitt claimed it would be totally different the next time the sides meet, in the World Cup.

At least Canada will not have to travel to Cardiff for their pool game, which is in Nantes, and will have a crop of players – unavailable in 2006 – for the World Cup.

"We will beat Wales, that's what we are going to the World Cup for," said Suggitt, after seeing his side lose 61–26 to Wales in Cardiff.

"It's a realistic aim and that's what we are building towards."

"This was a good experience for our guys, I asked them to be bold and throw caution to the wind, and when that happens mistakes can be made."

The Canucks stormed through their qualification rounds, almost embarrassing their near rivals, USA, with a massive 56–7 victory.

BOTH DEAN VAN CAMP AND BRODIE HENDERSON SCORED TRIES FOR CANADA IN 2003

Try machine heading for France

Japan may be targeting just one win in the 2007 World Cup but one thing is for sure: they will have a world record holder in their side, in the shape of Daisuke Ohata.

The wing scored his 69th test try when Japan romped through their qualification pool beating Hong Kong 52–3 and Korea 54–0 at the end of 2006.

Their improvement since 2003 is evident in those results, but a place in the quarter-finals still looks beyond them, even though they have recently appointed All Blacks legend John Kirwan as their coach.

"I am very pleased for the boys and Japan," said Kirwan. "There was lot of pressure on us before the game but we can now think about the World Cup. The players did their nation proud."

The Japanese will be strong contenders to host the 2015 World Cup, after just missing out – to New Zealand – for the 2011 event.

IN DAISUKE OHATA (TOP LEFT) JAPAN HAVE THE WORLD'S LEADING TRY SCORER, WHILE IN 2003 THEY HAD TAKASHI TSUJI (LEFT) AS SCRUM-HALF

POOL B Stadium

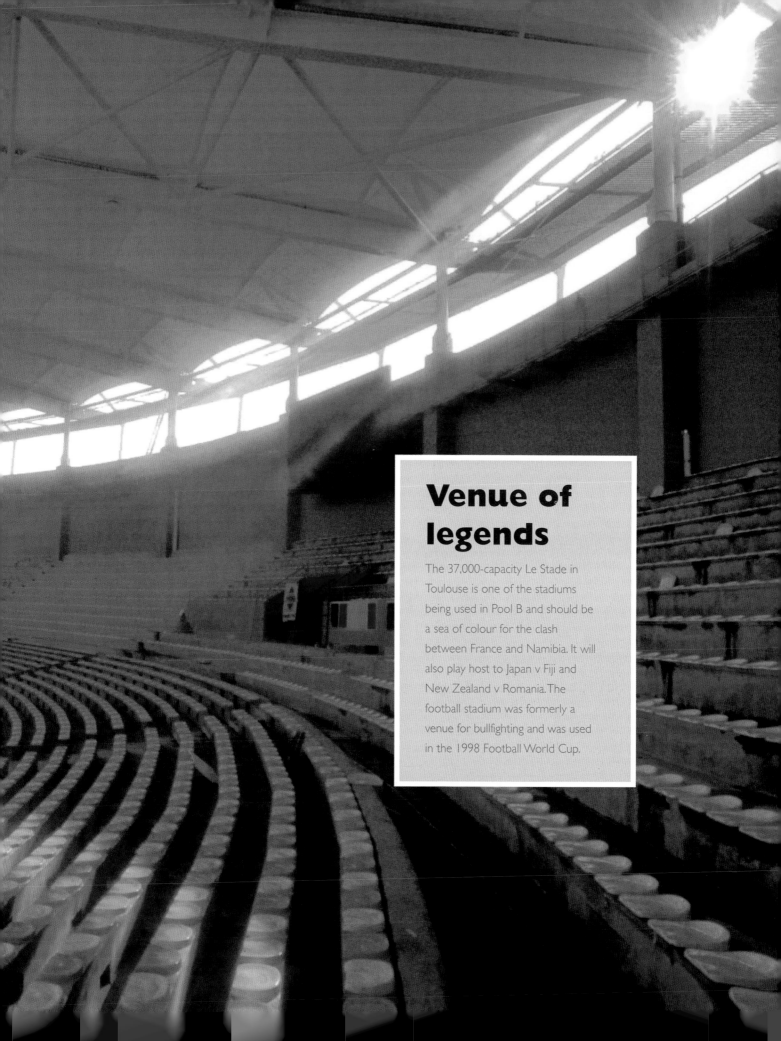

Venue of legends

The 37,000-capacity Le Stade in Toulouse is one of the stadiums being used in Pool B and should be a sea of colour for the clash between France and Namibia. It will also play host to Japan v Fiji and New Zealand v Romania. The football stadium was formerly a venue for bullfighting and was used in the 1998 Football World Cup.

Motoring to The World Cup

The New Zealand All Blacks will arrive at the 2007 World Cup as the hottest favourites in the history of the tournament, and it will be a major shock if they do not win. Over a two-year period they have broken records and stunned the opposition wherever they go. Only South Africa have beaten New Zealand in those 23 games and coach Graham Henry sees the Springboks as a big threat in 2007.

"South Africa will be a real challenge in the World Cup," said Henry. "They have got a lot of guys at home who didn't come on their European tour in 2006. I think Jake White (South Africa coach) got it right. They had a lot of young guys come through on the trip."

"And they are not intimidated by the All Blacks. They think they can handle us."

Henry has assembled not only a world-class playing squad but has brought in Steve Hansen (from Wales)

ANTON OLIVER (LEFT) IN NEW ZEALAND'S UNSUCCESSFUL 2003 CAMPAIGN, BUT FOUR YEARS LATER HE WILL BE HOPING TO GO ONE STAGE BETTER

and Wayne Smith (from Northampton) as his coaches. And in 2005 and 2006 Henry set about developing a squad of 30 players who could conquer the world. Henry was criticised for a rotation policy that saw a number of changes, although as his side kept winning he was able to keep going.

CHRIS MASOE (BELOW) AND CASEY LAULALA (ABOVE) ARE TWO ALL BLACKS WHO HAVE EMERGED IN THE LAST TWO YEARS AS THE ALL BLACKS BECAME THE WORLD'S NUMBER ONE SIDE

LUKE MCALISTER LEADS THE ALL BLACKS
THROUGH IRELAND'S DEFENCE AS THEY
STARTED THEIR 2006 SEASON WITH A
VICTORY. THEY NEVER LOOKED BACK,
LOSING JUST ONE MATCH IN THE YEAR,
AND THAT AFTER THEY HAD BEEN
CROWNED TRI-NATIONS CHAMPIONS

POOL C — NEW ZEALAND

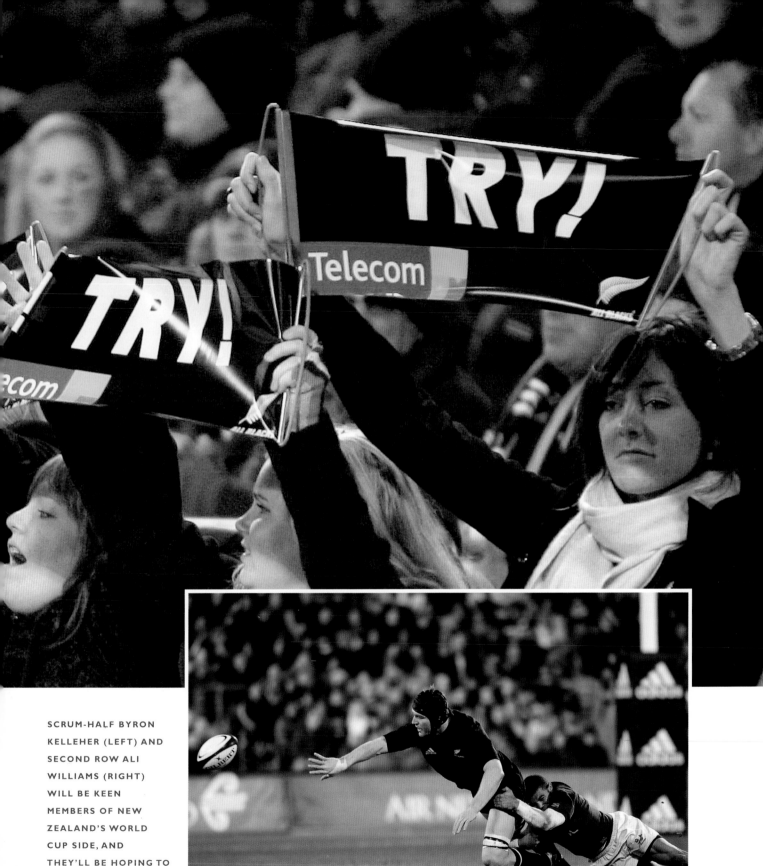

SCRUM-HALF BYRON KELLEHER (LEFT) AND SECOND ROW ALI WILLIAMS (RIGHT) WILL BE KEEN MEMBERS OF NEW ZEALAND'S WORLD CUP SIDE, AND THEY'LL BE HOPING TO KEEP THEIR LEGIONS OF SUPPORTERS IN GOOD VOICE

Scots head for France with hope in their hearts

France only clinched the 2006 RBS Six Nations crown on the final day of the championship, but there was no doubt over the title for the tournament's most-improved team – Scotland.

The Scots had endured one of the most miserable periods in their history either side of the 2003 World Cup, but along came new coach Frank Hadden in 2005 to turn round their fortunes and make them contenders for a place in the semi-finals this time around.

Scotland managed just one victory – over Italy – in two Six Nations tournaments under Australian Matt Williams, before Hadden took over. If we presume Scotland won't complete their first-ever win over New Zealand at the World Cup, even if the game is in Edinburgh, the key game for the Scots is likely to come in St-Étienne, on 29 September, when they take on Italy.

SEAN LAMONT (RIGHT) IS ONE OF THE MOST POTENT WEAPONS AT THE DISPOSAL OF SCOTLAND COACH FRANK HADDEN

POOL C – SCOTLAND

The fact that Frank Hadden's Scotland will already have played New Zealand could have a huge bearing on his selection. Many would favour a weakened side going out at Murrayfield to face New Zealand, saving the big guns for the Italy game that could guarantee them a quarter-final berth. Scotland did worry their fans a little with their final game of 2006, a 40–15 defeat at home to an Australian side that had already lost to Ireland and drawn with Wales. "It is an extremely young side, and that gives me tremendous confidence with the next World Cup looming in 2007," said Hadden. "Scotland's history has seen one or two occasions of tremendous over-achievement, and I am hoping this is the start of one for us."

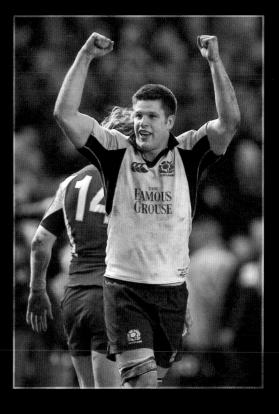

Azzurri aim to rattle the big boys

Italy started their build-up to the 2007 Rugby World Cup with an impressive set of performances a year before that will make them dangerous outsiders in France. The Italians will also be buoyed by an excellent recent record against World Cup opponents Scotland, completing their first Six Nations win in 2000 over them, and repeating the trick four years later. They had been the whipping boys of the Six Nations in between, but their fortunes have taken an upward curve since the appointment of Pierre Berbizier in 2005, taking over from John Kirwan. In November 2006 they lost to Argentina, pushed Australia hard and beat Canada 41–6.

Berbizier felt the 18–18 draw against Wales in the 2006 RBS Six Nations was a big breakthrough for his side. "This gives a mark of respect for the Italian team on the international scene," Berbizier said. "To hold Wales here is a big achievement and we now have the respect of the other teams. We are now showing what we are capable of achieving."

Italy became the seventh side to qualify for the 2007 World Cup, with a convincing 67–7 result against Russia.

MAURO BERGAMASCO (RIGHT) AND CAPTAIN MARCO BORTOLAMI (CENTRE, WITH HEAD GUARD) LEAD AN EVER-GROWING LIST OF WORLD-CLASS PLAYERS IN THE ITALIAN SIDE, MAKING THEM A TEAM WHO COULD CAUSE A SHOCK IN 2007

PABLO CANAVOSIO SCORES AND THEN CELEBRATES A TRY AS ITALY CLAIMED THEIR FIRST-EVER AWAY POINT IN THE SIX NATIONS, DRAWING 18–18 WITH WALES IN 2006

Life is tough for the minnows

Romania will be dangerous foes for Scotland, having beaten them twice, in 1984 and 1991, and coming into the tournament as European Nations Cup (Second Division of the Six Nations) champions. Romania's chances of staging an upset have been hampered by the decision to stage the match at Murrayfield. How much more even would this game be if it was staged in Marseille or Bordeaux? Instead the minnows are dealt yet another bad hand by the organisers, and left to travel to the home of Scottish rugby, to face Scotland in a World Cup match!

LUCIAN SIRBU AND OVIDIU TONITA OF ROMANIA (ABOVE) CELEBRATE WINNING THE WORLD CUP POOL MATCH AGAINST NAMIBIA IN 2003, WHERE THEY WERE LED BY CAPTAIN ROMEO GONTINEAC (BELOW) AND IN FRANCE THEY WILL FACE PORTUGAL WHO QUALIFIED FOR THE FIRST TIME

POOL C – ROMANIA

The final finalists

Portugal – coached by Tomaz Morais – became the twentieth and last side to qualify for the World Cup with a thrilling, two-leg, 24–23 victory over Uruguay.

DESPITE LOSING THE SECOND LEG IN MONTEVIDEO (BELOW) THE PORTUGUESE PLAYERS CELEBRATE AN HISTORIC VICTORY WITH AN OVERALL AGGREGATE ADVANTAGE OF JUST ONE POINT, ENOUGH TO TAKE THEM TO THE FINALS

POOL C

Portugal

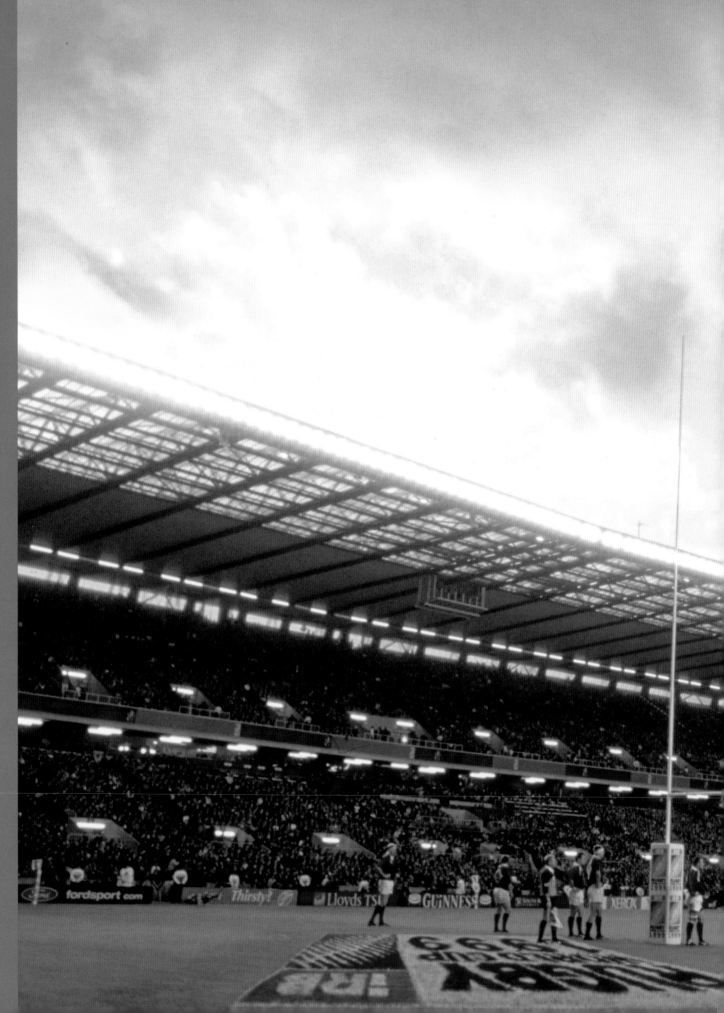

Magnificent Murrayfield

Murrayfield, the home of Scottish rugby will be home to two matches in the World Cup, including the crucial Scotland v New Zealand clash on 23 September. The stadium now holds 67,500 fans, after being reopened in 1994 following a redevelopment costing £37million. It still holds the record for the biggest attendance at a rugby game, when a crowd of 104,000 watched Scotland play Wales in 1975.

France

POOL D

YANNICK JAUZION
(ABOVE), DESCRIBED BY
SOME AS THE WORLD'S
BEST PLAYER, HAS THE
ABILITY TO MASTERMIND
FRANCE'S FIRST RUGBY
WORLD CUP TITLE

FRANCE'S PLAYMAKER,
FRÉDÉRIC MICHALAK
(RIGHT) WILL BE CRUCIAL
TO FRANCE'S EFFORTS,
MISSING A HUGE PART OF
THE 2006–07 SEASON
AFTER INJURING HIS KNEE
IN NOVEMBER 2006

60

POOL D – FRANCE

France look to capitalise on their home advantage

The most successful northern hemisphere country in the history of the Rugby World Cup, France, will be straining every sinew to go one better than their appearance in the 1987 final.

Since that epic final 20 years ago, France have only once failed to make at least the semi-final, in 1991, pulling off a series of breathtaking wins in the last four finals.

Their most memorable was the 43–31 victory over New Zealand in 1999 as they fell behind before scoring 33 points to seven from the All Blacks to storm home.

In 2003 England were their semi-final conquerors, beating Les Bleus 24–7, but since that time France have won a Grand Slam and an RBS Six Nations Championship.

In the November 2006 matches France suffered two morale-sapping defeats to New Zealand, yet finished off the series with a win over Argentina.

But coach Bernard Laporte is urging his side to go back to their roots for the World Cup, and show the flair which makes them famous – and feared – throughout the rugby world.

"The intentions are all there, but we need to be more ambitious. We need to let ourselves go more," says Laporte, who knows his side have the honour of playing in the first match of the World Cup, against Argentina.

"The All Blacks are definitely above the rest but, hopefully, the World Cup will be another story than this November tour."

Team Manager Jo Maso added: "We went into the game (against Argentina) with two objectives, to win and to win in style. We won and we played with style for an hour, now we have to work to keep the rhythm for a whole match."

FRANCE'S MAGNIFICENT FANS WILL BE IN GOOD VOICE AND COLOURFULLY DRESSED FOR THE WORLD CUP, AND WILL BE HOPING TO SEE PLAYERS LIKE DAMIEN TRAILLE (LEFT) AND FLORIAN FRITZ CELEBRATING SOME GREAT TRIES

THE TWO YANNICKS, NYANGA (LEFT) AND JAUZION (RIGHT) HAVE THE ABILITY TO BE THE HEARTBEAT OF THE FRANCE TEAM AT THIS WORLD CUP. NYANGA IS ONE OF THE BRIGHTEST PROSPECTS IN EUROPEAN RUGBY, WHILE JAUZION HAS THE CAPABILITY TO MASTERMIND THE FRANCE WORLD CUP CAMPAIGN

Ireland ripe for a cracking World Cup

In Ireland's history there have been many great days. The Grand Slam of 1948, the recent Triple Crowns of 2004 and 2006, but there aren't too many dates competing for the worst day – most people would accept that was on 20 October, 1999. On that day Ireland were forced to travel to Lens for a quarter-final play-off against Argentina on a night of high drama. Ireland lost that game, 28–24, and their place in the world's top-eight countries. Reputations were ruined on that fateful night in northern France and the Irish even had to suffer the embarrassment of being forced to qualify for the 2003 tournament. It means that even to this day, Ireland are one nation that will never underestimate the Argentinians.

Ireland face the Argentinians again in 2007 but this time as one of the form nations in the northern hemisphere, confirmed by a magnificent and unbeaten run in November 2006.

Australia, South Africa and the Pacific Islanders all arrived in Dublin and were all beaten comprehensively.

Those victories left Ireland as the world's third best side, according to the IRB Rankings, leaving coach Eddie O'Sullivan trying his best to play down his side's World Cup hopes.

"It was a good victory against a strong Australia team. They weren't experimenting and put their best foot forward for this game," said O'Sullivan. "I don't take too much notice of where we are in the game. It doesn't change where you are in the overall scheme of things."

"The rankings are a barometer of where a team are. You can only draw conclusions from it over a period of time."

"Ireland have been in and around the top five for the last couple of years. We are third now but if we lost a couple of games we'd slip right back down."

IRELAND HAVE ESTABLISHED THEMSELVES AS ONE OF THE WORLD'S BEST SIDES UNDER THE CAPTAINCY OF BRIAN O'DRISCOLL

SHANE HORGAN IS ONE OF THE MOST
IMPROVED PLAYERS IN A POTENT IRELAND
BACKLINE THAT COULD CAUSE A SHOCK OR
TWO AT THE WORLD CUP. HERE HE LEAVES
DAFYDD JAMES ON THE GROUND AS HE ELUDES
THE WELSH DEFENCE TO SCORE A TRY AT
LANDSDOWNE ROAD IN THE RBS SIX NATIONS

Beware the dangerous Los Pumas

Of all the outsiders in this Rugby World Cup, it is the Argentinians who are most likely to give the so-called 'big boys' a bloody nose. They have a history of upsets from their quarter-final play-off victory over Ireland in 1999 to the victory over world champions England, at Twickenham, in 2006. That win left Argentina ranked as the seventh best side in the world. For a side made up almost exclusively of European-based players, France will seem like a home from home. They will kick off the 2007 World Cup, playing hosts France, as they did in 1999 and 2003. Led by inspirational captain Agustin Pichot, the Pumas hope that another impressive World Cup campaign will lead to them being admitted to either the RBS Six Nations or Tri-Nations Championship, after 2006 wins over England and Italy. "I think that the rugby people must think about Argentina. Our current performance justifies our inclusion in the main international tournaments." said Pichot. Who could deny him?

GONZALO TIESI (ABOVE RIGHT), SCORING AGAINST WALES, IS ONE OF A GROWING NUMBER OF ARGENTINIAN PLAYERS FROM THE GUINNESS PREMIERSHIP, WHILE (RIGHT) FEDERICO MARTIN ARAMBURU CRASHES OVER FOR A TRY AGAINST WORLD CUP OPPONENTS IRELAND. BELOW ARGENTINA TAKE ON NEW ZEALAND IN JUNE 2006, COMING CLOSE TO BEATING THE ALL BLACKS, FINALLY LOSING 25–19

Third time lucky for the Namibians

No one could question Namibia's place at the 2007 World Cup. Despite losing by record margins in 2003 they completed one of the most torturous routes to this year's tournaments, finally emerging as the best side in Africa, behind the Springboks. After clearing a number of qualifying hurdles, they finally clinched their place with a two-leg

NAMIBIA CAPTAIN KEES LENSING IS LOOKING FORWARD TO LEADING HIS SIDE INTO THIS YEAR'S WORLD CUP, HOPEFULLY AVOIDING SOME OF THE HAMMERINGS THEY TOOK IN 2003

victory over Morocco in Windhoek, securing a 52–15 aggregate victory.

"I am delighted that we have achieved our goal of qualifying for the Rugby World Cup 2007," said Namibia captain Kees Lensing. "Knowing that Morocco would throw everything at us we could not afford to defend our advantage. Therefore, I am really pleased that we played some positive rugby and scored four tries in the process."

Let's go round again

There were scenes of jubilation in Lisbon when Georgia became the 18th team to qualify for the 2007 World Cup, after winning their two-legged battle with Portugal. The sides drew 11–11 in the Portugese capital, but the Georgians' 14-point lead from that first leg booked their World Cup place.

The Georgians made their World Cup debut in 2003, qualifying into England and South Africa's group in Australia.

They failed to win a game in 2003, but their presence in Australia was a breath of fresh air.

"We need experience. We are a baby," said Zara Kassachvili, the vice-president of the Georgian federation.

THE GEORGIA TEAM (TOP) CELEBRATE THEIR WIN OVER PORTUGAL WHILE PLAYERS DAVIT ZIRAKASHVILI (LEFT) AND MAMUKA GORGODZE SHOW HOW ELATED THEY ARE TO QUALIFY FOR THE WORLD CUP

The jewel of southern France

The southernmost city to stage matches at the Rugby World Cup, Marseilles will be a sea of rugby on the weekend of October 6 and 7 as the famous football stadium hosts two quarter-finals, deciding the fate of the sides in all four pools.

Earlier in the tournament New Zealand and Italy will do battle in the French port, while France will visit there on 30 September to take on the Georgians.

PART
heroes in

FROM BORTOLAMI TO WHITE...THE MEN SET TO MAKE

TWO
waiting

THE HEADLINES AT THE 2007 RUGBY WORLD CUP

MARCO BORTOLAMI – Second row – Italy A large part of the rugby world is dying for one of the so-called smaller nations to make the breakthrough into the quarter-finals of the Rugby World Cup. Italy is one of the nations on the verge of that breakthrough, one of the reasons being their charismatic and imposing leader, Marco Bortolami. A lineout expert, Bortolami became Italy's youngest captain when he led his country against Japan in 2004. Bortolami was a crucial absentee when Italy played Wales for a place in the 2003 World Cup quarter-finals, but this time around his experience – after moving to Gloucester in the summer of 2006 – will be crucial to their hopes.

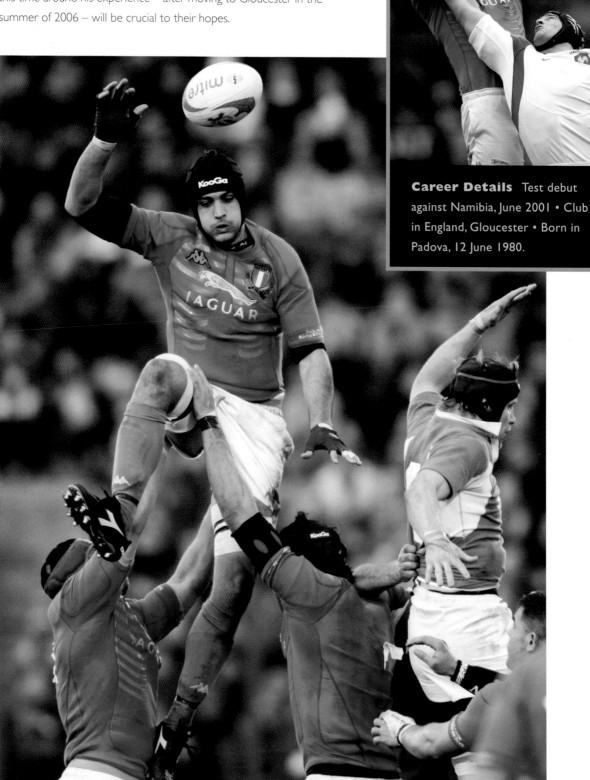

Career Details Test debut against Namibia, June 2001 • Club in England, Gloucester • Born in Padova, 12 June 1980.

Career Details Test debut against England, June 2003 • Province, in New Zealand, The Crusaders • Born in Leeston, 5 March 1982.

CALLING MR WONDERFUL... THE WORLD'S BEST PLAYER IN 2005, DAN CARTER WILL BE CRUCIAL TO NEW ZEALAND'S CHANCES AT THE WORLD CUP

BREAKTHROUGH BOYS... IS THIS THE TOURNAMENT WHEN MARCO BORTOLAMI'S (OPPOSITE) ITALY WILL MAKE THEIR FIRST MOVE INTO THE QUARTER-FINALS?

DAN CARTER – Outside-half – New Zealand

In every generation come players who can mesmerise, change the course of a game, or even a World Cup. Such a player – in 2007 – is the Canterbury Crusader, Dan Carter. The outside-half first announced himself on the world stage in 2005 when his performances with the boot – and with ball in hand – were a big factor in New Zealand's record-breaking series win over the Lions. An exemplary goalkicker, he made his debut, aged 21, against Wales in 2003, scoring 20 points, and in his first 30 Tests he averaged almost 16 points a game.

HEROES IN WAITING

79

RUPENI CAUCAUNIBUCA – Wing – Fiji At the last two World Cups
the quarter-finalists have been almost exactly the same eight teams. So if one of
the so-called minnows is going to make a breakthrough in 2007 it will need some
of the ability of Fiji's Rupeni Caucaunibuca to lead the charge. Caucau as he is
better known is a mould-breaking runner, tough to stop – with his powerful frame
– and with an enviable turn of speed, which sees him complete the 100 metres in
less than 11 seconds.

ROCKET MAN...RUPENI CAUCAUNIBUCA, OR CAUCAU TO
HIS FRIENDS, MADE A HUGE IMPACT IN 2003. WATCH OUT
FOR HIS OWN BRAND OF FIREWORKS IN 2007

HEROES IN WAITING

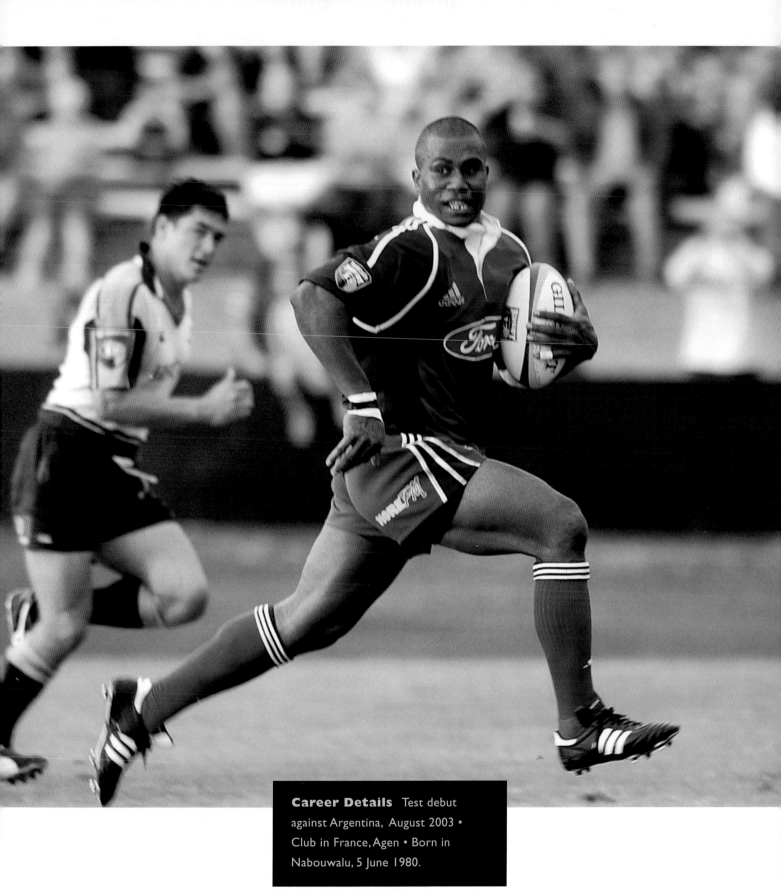

Career Details Test debut against Argentina, August 2003 • Club in France, Agen • Born in Nabouwalu, 5 June 1980.

FOURIE DU PREEZ – Scrum-half – South Africa

When the shortlist for the International Rugby Board's Player of the Year was announced in 2006, one player's presence caused a few eyebrows to be raised. Joining players like Richie McCaw, Dan Carter and Paul O'Connell was Springboks' scrum-half Fourie Du Preez, a player who made a huge impact in 2006 when he made the South African number nine shirt his own. A speed merchant from the base of the scrum, Du Preez has a quick pass that is capable of getting any backline moving. Du Preez only made his Super 12 debut – for the Bulls – in 2003, making his debut for South Africa a year later, such was his initial impact on the game. At the end of the 2006 Tri-Nations he announced himself on the world stage with tries against New Zealand in both Wellington and Pretoria, proving his ability to break down the most impressive defence in the world.

Career Details Test debut against Ireland, June 2004 • Province in South Africa, Blue Bulls • Born in Pretoria, 24 March 1982.

LIGHTNING FIRE... FOURIE DU PREEZ BURST ONTO THE INTERNATIONAL SCENE IN 2006. WATCH HIM GO WHEN THE SPRINGBOKS TOUCH DOWN IN FRANCE

82

HEROES IN WAITING

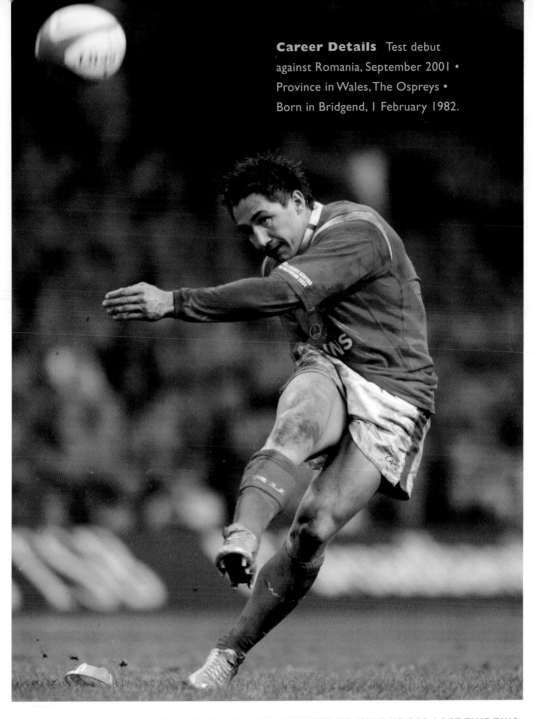

Gavin Henson – Wales

BOOT BOY... HENSON MISSED OUT IN 2003. HE'S DESTINED TO MAKE UP FOR LOST TIME THIS TIME AROUND

GAVIN HENSON – **Centre** – **Wales** When Gavin Henson stepped up to land a monster penalty against England in 2005, his place in Welsh folk history was guaranteed. Not only did the nerveless 45-metre kick ensure an 11–9 win but it set Wales on course for their first Grand Slam in 27 years. Another star who can play international rugby outside-half, centre or full-back, Henson was the International Rugby Board's Young Player of the Year in 2001. A solid defender, his deft touch with ball in hand sets him apart. An awful 2005–06 season when Henson was blighted by injury and suspension interrupted his impressive career, which had seen him help the Ospreys to the Celtic League title in 2005, and saw him make his Lions debut in New Zealand.

Yannick Jauzion – France

YANNICK JAUZION – **Centre** – **France**   Most rugby players would settle for speed, flair or the ability to make bulldozing runs. Yannick Jauzion, the France centre, manages all three. He emerged onto the world stage as a key part of the Toulouse side that reached the Heineken Cup final in 2003, 2004 and 2005. Jauzion – a destructive passer who can open up any defence – missed the 2006 RBS Six Nations through injury, but was an integral part of the France team that won Grand Slams in 2002 and 2004.

SIMPLY THE BEST…
ACCLAIMED BY
MANY AS THE
WORLD'S BEST
PLAYER, NOW IS
THE TIME FOR
YANNICK JAUZION
TO PROVE IT

Career Details   Test debut against South Africa, June 2001 • Club in France, Toulouse • Born in Graulhet, 28 July 1978.

CHRIS LATHAM – Full-back – Australia A full-back with devastating ability, Chris Latham won the ultimate honour in Australian rugby – in 2006 – after being awarded the John Eales Medal. Latham – who made his debut in 1998 – was the first back to receive the award, voted for by the Australian players. When he takes the field in France it will be his third World Cup. A gifted runner, Latham runs the angles that most rugby players can only dream of. The Queensland Red was voted Australian Super 12 Player of the Year three times, in 2000, 2003 and 2004.

FLYING HIGH... WITHOUT PEER IN THE AUSTRALIAN TEAM, THE WORLD CUP IS COMING AT THE PERFECT TIME FOR CHRIS LATHAM

Chris Latham – Australia

Career Details Test debut against France, November 1998 • Province, in Australia, The Queensland Reds • Born in Narrabri, 8 September 1975.

Josh Lewsey – England

JOSH LEWSEY – Full back/Wing – England After England won the World Cup in 2003 their squad suffered a minor disintegration. Players like captain Martin Johnson, Neil Back and Jason Leonard retired, and Jonny Wilkinson sustained a series of long-term injuries as England slipped to seventh in the world rankings. In the ensuing years there were countless changes but one man remained; Josh Lewsey. The London Wasps full back was the only player to be selected in the 22 Tests following the World Cup victory. At home either on the wing or at full back, Lewsey is a former army officer cadet, who struggled to balance life as a professional rugby player with that of a soldier. Lewsey made his debut on the infamous Tour to Hell undertaken by England in 1998, when they were thumped by Australia, New Zealand and South Africa. That trip was the making of players like Lewsey and Jonny Wilkinson. Unflappable under the high ball, Lewsey's pace and powerful running style make him one of the best finishers in the rugby world.

ENGLANDS MR RELIABLE, JOSH LEWSEY... EVADES THE TACKLE OF BRYAN HABANA (RIGHT) AND LEAVES DEFENDERS STANDING (BELOW) DURING A BRACE OF GAMES AGAINST POOL A RIVALS SOUTH AFRICA AT TWICKENHAM AT THE END OF 2006. ENGLAND WON THE FIRST ENCOUNTER AND SOUTH AFRICA THE SECOND

Career Details Test debut against New Zealand, June 1998 • Club in England, London Wasps • Born in Bromley, 30 November 1976.

BRIAN LIMA – Utility-back –

Samoa Most rugby players see playing in the Rugby World Cup as the culmination of their careers. But in 2007 Brian Lima looks certain to become the first man to play in an incredible five World Cups. Lima was on duty when Samoa turned the rugby world on its head – in 1991 – when they beat Wales in Cardiff and he'll be there again to take on England this time around. Nicknamed The Chiropractor because of his ability to make bone-crunching tackles, Lima is an on-field leader who inspires his side and can turn a game with one of his legendary big hits. Lima was the youngest player at the 1991 tournament and could now be the oldest, 16 years later, never having missed a World Cup match for his beloved Samoa.

HIT PARADE... BRIAN LIMA MAY BE ARRIVING AT THE WORLD CUP AS ONE OF THE OLD MEN BUT HE CAN STILL HIT WITH THE BEST AS DERICK HOUGAARD FOUND OUT IN 2003 (BELOW)

89

Career Details Test debut against Ireland, November 2001 • Province, in New Zealand, The Crusaders • Born in Oamaru, 31 December 1980.

RICHIE McCAW – Openside flanker – New Zealand When the voting closed for the IRB Player of the Year 2006, one thing was certain: Richie McCaw would be the winner. Of course there was a shortlist of five, but no one in the rugby world actually considered that they would vote for anyone else. The New Zealand skipper is the key to the All Blacks' hopes at the World Cup. If he rules the roost at the breakdown, they have the backs to beat any side in the world.

RAMPANT RICHIE... HAS THERE BEEN A BETTER NO 7 IN THE HISTORY OF THE GAME? WE'LL FIND OUT AT THE WORLD CUP

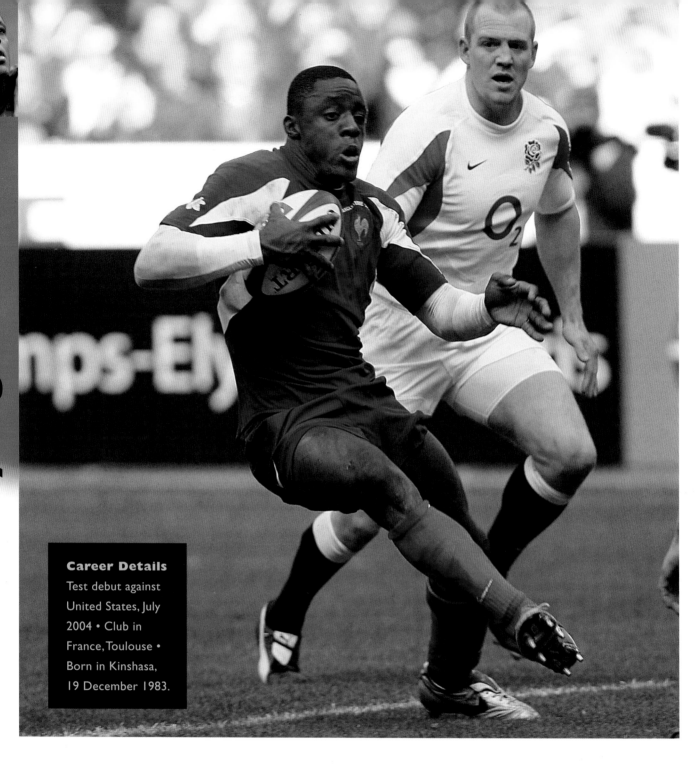

Yannick Nyanga – France

Career Details
Test debut against United States, July 2004 • Club in France, Toulouse • Born in Kinshasa, 19 December 1983.

YANNICK NYANGA – Openside flanker – France France has a long and successful tradition of African-born sportsmen and women starring in their national sides. Think of Serge Betsen in the 2003 World Cup or Marie-José Pérec striding to three Olympic golds in the 1990s. The latest in a long line of Africans to move into the France rugby team is the dynamic Yannick Nyanga, who was born in the Democratic Republic of the Congo, but now plays for Toulouse. He only made his debut in 2004, but his athletic ability and rock-solid defence quickly marked him out as a world star.

STAR IN THE MAKING... YANNICK NYANGA HAS COME FROM OBSCURITY – IN THE LAST FOUR YEARS – TO MAKE THE FRENCH TEAM. BUT AS ENGLAND FOUND OUT IN 2006 (ABOVE) HE HAS THE ABILITY TO LIVE WITH THE BEST

92

HEROES IN WAITING

PAUL O'CONNELL – **Second row –**

Ireland Any side looking to make an impact at the 2007 World Cup will need men of strength in the pack and the greatest example could be found in the green of Ireland. Paul O'Connell is a second row forward to rival any on the planet. A man of Munster, O'Connell made his Ireland debut in 2002, establishing himself on the world stage at the World Cup the following year. Guaranteed to win his own ball at lineout time, O'Connell is a big threat on opposition ball, a fearsome scrummager and a real danger in the loose.

THE O TEAM... PAUL O'CONNELL IS HITTING FORM JUST IN TIME TO BE A COLOSSUS AT THE 2007 WORLD CUP

Career Details
Test debut against Wales, February 2002 • Province in Ireland, Munster • Born in Limerick, 20 October 1979.

Paul O'Connell – Ireland

IN BOD WE TRUST... BRIAN O'DRISCOLL IS ONE OF THE STARS OF EUROPEAN RUGBY. THE WORLD CUP PRESENTS HIM WITH THE CHANCE TO BECOME A WORLD GREAT

Career Details Test debut against Australia, June 1999 • Province in Ireland, Leinster • Born in Dublin, 21 January 1979.

BRIAN O'DRISCOLL – Centre – Ireland Every side needs their talisman and if Ireland are going to have a successful 2007 World Cup campaign, captain Brian O'Driscoll will have to hit some of the best form of his career. A sensational player for both Leinster and Ireland, O'Driscoll had the unenviable task of taking over the national captaincy from the legendary Keith Wood – in 2003 – and the Leinster man led them to Triple Crowns in 2004 and 2006. He made his Ireland debut in 1999 and quickly established himself as a world star, his elusive running style bringing him a hat trick against France, in Paris in 2000, as his side won 27–25. He was made Lions captain in 2005, but survived less than two minutes of the first test, missing the rest of the tour with a career-threatening shoulder injury.

HEROES IN WAITING

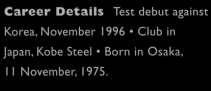

Career Details Test debut against Korea, November 1996 • Club in Japan, Kobe Steel • Born in Osaka, 11 November, 1975.

DAISUKE OHATA – Wing – Japan

Only two players in the history of rugby union have scored more than 60 tries in Test matches. One is the famous David Campese while the other is Japanese speedster Daisuke Ohata. The Japan wing overtook Campese's world record – which had stood for ten years – in May 2006 when he scored three tries against Georgia. A wing or occasionally a centre, Ohata – who plays for Kobe Steel in the Japanese Top League – captained Japan when they won the Asian qualifying tournament in November 2006, to make it to the 2007 World Cup.

TRY MACHINE... DAISUKE OHATA WILL STRETCH HIS LEAD OVER THE WORLD'S BEST AT THE WORLD CUP

Career Details Test debut against Japan, May 1995 • Club in France, Toulouse • Born in Ogwr, 27 July 1974.

HEROES IN WAITING

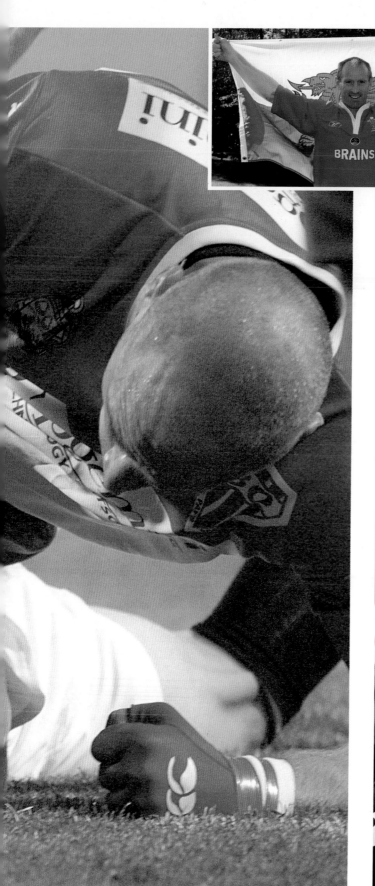

**GARETH THOMAS –
Utility back – Wales** No
Wales rugby player has
scored more international
tries than the man
affectionately called Alfie
Thomas the length and
breadth of the country.
Thomas made his Wales
debut against Japan in 1995
and went on to play in three World Cups, captaining his
country in 2003, in Australia. Equally at home in the centre,
on the wing or at full-back, he has been a crucial part of
the Wales set-up. Thomas started his career at his
hometown club Bridgend, moving on to Celtic Warriors,
Cardiff and Toulouse. He lost the Wales captaincy in 2006,
after battling back from a health scare that threatened his
career when he suffered a ruptured artery in his neck.

WELSH WARRIOR... THOMAS EPITOMISES THE SPIRIT OF
THE WELSH NATION WHETHER IN THE WHITE OF
TOULOUSE (LEFT) OR WITH THE DRAGON ABOVE HIS
HEAD (ABOVE)

Jason White – Scotland

Career Details Test debut against England, April 2000 • Club in England, Sale Sharks • Born in Edinburgh, 17 April 1978.

THE FAMOUS GROUSE

JASON WHITE – **Blindside flanker –
Scotland** It is no coincidence that the
letters that make up the word HIT
figure prominently in the name Jason
White. The unassuming Scotland
captain was the key reason for the
country's re-emergence in 2006,
when they beat both world
champions England and Six Nations
Championship winners France. One of
the best blindside flankers in the world, he
is famous for his steamroller tackles, and
renowned as one of the hardest hitters in the
rugby world. A big threat at the back of the lineout,
he played a crucial part in Sale winning the first
English championship in their history, in 2006.
The Scotland Player of the Year in 2005–06, his
turnovers have the capability of turning matches.

FLOWER OF SCOTLAND... JASON WHITE HAS
HELPED RESTORE THE PRIDE BACK TO THE
SCOTLAND TEAM AND THEY TURN OUT TO BE ONE
OF THE DARK HORSES FOR THE WORLD CUP

PART

the path to

WINNERS OF THE PREVIOUS FIVE WORLD CUP EVENTS

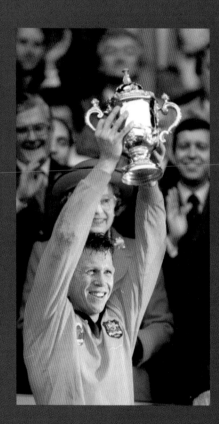

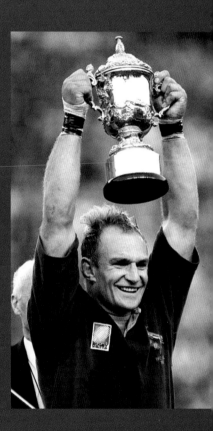

**1987
NEW
ZEALAND**

**1991
AUSTRALIA**

**1995
SOUTH
AFRICA**

THREE
glory
COMPLETE WITH ALL THE ESSENTIAL STATISTICS

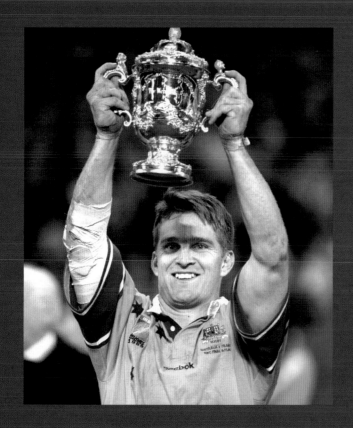

**1999
AUSTRALIA**

**2003
ENGLAND**

The All Blacks first to conquer

The Rugby world was a very different place in 1987, but some things don't change as the New Zealand All Blacks were confirmed as the best team in the world, lifting the Webb Ellis Cup for the first time.

In a tournament staged in New Zealand and Australia the All Blacks stormed through the competition scoring an impressive 298 points in their six games and never seriously being troubled once. France got closest to beating David Kirk's team, but even they succumbed by 20 points in the final.

Grant Fox stood like a colossus over this first World Cup, scoring 126 points – a record that still stands today.

"Lifting the cup was how people must feel at the top of Everest. They only have 20 minutes there and won't ever be back," said Kirk. "The only way back is down. But that melancholy was overwhelmed by joy."

Wales were the leading Home Nation, finishing third, a position they failed to beat in the following four tournaments. The 16 sides who competed were invited, rather than having to qualify as they to do today.

ROBERT JONES OF WALES CLEARS HIS LINES AS THE WELSH OVERCOME AUSTRALIA FOR THIRD PLACE (ABOVE)

ENGLAND STARTED THE FIRST WORLD CUP BADLY, LOSING 19–6 TO AUSTRALIA (RIGHT). A DISAPPOINTING TOURNAMENT FOR ENGLAND ENDED WHEN THEY WERE BEATEN IN THE QUARTER-FINALS BY WALES

THE NEW ZEALAND TEAM
PERFORM THE HAKA
PRIOR TO THEIR SEMI-
FINAL CLASH WITH
WALES (ABOVE)

NEW ZEALAND CAPTAIN
DAVID KIRK CRASHES
OVER IN THE FINAL (LEFT)
AND LATER LIFTS THE
TROPHY FOLLOWING THE
ALL BLACKS' 29–9
VICTORY OVER FRANCE
(RIGHT)

NEW ZEALAND 1987

1987 Stat Attack

The Pool Stages

POOL A

AUSTRALIA	19–6	ENGLAND
JAPAN	18–21	USA
ENGLAND	60–7	JAPAN
AUSTRALIA	47–12	USA
ENGLAND	34–6	USA
AUSTRALIA	42–23	JAPAN

POOL B

CANADA	37–4	TONGA
IRELAND	6–13	WALES
WALES	29–16	TONGA
IRELAND	46–19	CANADA
WALES	40–9	CANADA
IRELAND	32–9	TONGA

POOL C

NEW ZEALAND	70–6	ITALY
FIJI	28–9	ARGENTINA
NEW ZEALAND	74–13	FIJI
ARGENTINA	25–16	ITALY
FIJI	15–18	ITALY
N ZEALAND	46–15	ARGENTINA

POOL D

ROMANIA	21–20	ZIMBABWE
FRANCE	20–20	SCOTLAND
FRANCE	55–12	ROMANIA
SCOTLAND	60–21	ZIMBABWE
FRANCE	70–12	ZIMBABWE
SCOTLAND	55–28	ROMANIA

THE KNOCKOUT STAGES
QUARTER-FINALS

NEW ZEALAND	30–3	SCOTLAND
FRANCE	31–16	FIJI
AUSTRALIA	33–15	IRELAND
WALES	16–3	ENGLAND

SEMI-FINALS

AUSTRALIA	24–30	FRANCE
NEW ZEALAND	49–6	WALES

THIRD-PLACE MATCH
AUSTRALIA 21–22 WALES

THE 1987 WORLD CUP FINAL
NEW ZEALAND 29–9 FRANCE

NEW ZEALAND
J GALLAGHER, J KIRWAN, W TAYLOR,
J STANLEY, C GREEN, G FOX, D KIRK
(CAPT), S MCDOWELL, S FITZPATRICK,
J DRAKE, G WHETTON, M PIERCE,
A WHETTON, M JONES, W SHELFORD

SCORERS
TRIES JONES, KIRK, KIRWAN **CONS** FOX
PENS FOX 4 **DROP GOALS** FOX

FRANCE
S BLANCO, D CAMBERABERO, P SELLA,
D CHARVET, P LAGISQUET, F MESNEL,
P BERBIZIER, P ONDARTS, D DUBROCA
(CAPT), JP GARUET, J CONDOM,
A LORIEUX, D ERBANI, E CHAMP,
L RODRIGUEZ

SCORERS
TRIES BERBIZIER **CONS** CAMBERABERO
PENS CAMBERABERO

1987 WORLD CUP RECORDS

MOST POINTS
126 G FOX (NZ), 82 M LYNAGH (AUS)
62 G HASTINGS (SCOT)

MOST TRIES
6 C GREEN (NZ), 6 J KIRWAN (NZ)

MOST DROP GOALS
3 J DAVIES (WALES)

MOST POINTS IN A MATCH
30 D CAMBERABERO (FRANCE V
ZIMBABWE), 27 G HASTINGS (SCOTLAND V
ROMANIA), 26 G FOX (NZ V FIJI)

AUSTRALIA, WITH DAVID CAMPESE (TOP) IN
GREAT FORM, ENJOYED A BREATHTAKING
QUARTER-FINAL AGAINST IRELAND, BEFORE
GOING ON TO LIFT THE CUP. AGAINST
IRELAND THEY FELL BEHIND TO A LATE

GORDON HAMILTON TRY BUT IN INJURY TIME
MICHAEL LYNAGH (ABOVE) STOLE THE SHOW
WITH A SENSATIONAL SCORE, WHILE
SCOTLAND AND DAVID SOLE (RIGHT) LOST
9–6 TO ENGLAND IN THE SEMI-FINAL

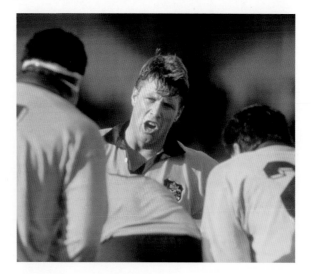

Wallabies climb to rugby's summit

After two countries hosted the first World Cup it was decided to bring the second tournament to the northern hemisphere and share it amongst the five nations of Wales, England, Scotland, Ireland and France. England hosted the first game – which they lost to New Zealand – and due to the pool system were also around at the end, managing to achieve the unique distinction of also losing the last – the final – to Australia.

In between, Will Carling's England endured one of the most tortuous routes to any World Cup final, having to beat France – in Paris – and Scotland – in Edinburgh – to make it.

But in that final – when the 1991 competition's one millionth spectator came through the turnstiles – they were kidded by David Campese and his fellow Wallabies to abandon their narrow game plan, that relied on their juggernaut pack, to play a more expansive style …and right into the hands of Australia.

In the final Australia, captained by Nick Farr-Jones (above), got home courtesy of one try, from Tony Daly.

New Zealand failed in their attempt to win back-to-back titles, losing to Australia in the semi-finals.

Ireland's Ralph Keyes ended as the tournament's leading scorer with 68 points.

AUSTRALIA CAPTAIN NICK FARR-JONES DECLARED IT "A DREAM COME TRUE" WHEN HE LIFTED THE WEBB ELLIS CUP (LEFT) JUST BEFORE HE AND HIS TEAM-MATES DIVED INTO THE BATHS AT TWICKENHAM (BELOW) BRINGING THE TROPHY WITH THEM! "EVERYTHING YOU'VE EVER DONE IN RUGBY BECOMES WORTHWHILE WHEN YOU WIN THE WORLD CUP – AND WHAT WE SHOWED WAS ALL ABOUT COURAGE," FARR-JONES ADDED AFTER THE 12–6 VICTORY OVER ENGLAND IN THE FINAL

1991 Stat Attack

The Pool Stages

POOL A

NEW ZEALAND	18–12	ENGLAND
ITALY	30–9	USA
NEW ZEALAND	46–6	USA
ENGLAND	36–6	ITALY
ENGLAND	37–9	USA
NEW ZEALAND	31–21	ITALY

POOL B

SCOTLAND	47–9	JAPAN
IRELAND	55–11	ZIMBABWE
IRELAND	32–16	JAPAN
SCOTLAND	51–12	ZIMBABWE
SCOTLAND	24–15	IRELAND
JAPAN	52–8	ZIMBABWE

POOL C

AUSTRALIA	32–19	ARGENTINA
WESTERN SAMOA	16–13	WALES
AUSTRALIA	9–3	WESTERN SAMOA
WALES	16–7	ARGENTINA
AUSTRALIA	38–3	WALES
WESTERN SAMOA	35–12	ARGENTINA

POOL D

FRANCE	30–3	ROMANIA
CANADA	13–3	FIJI
FRANCE	33–9	FIJI
CANADA	19–11	ROMANIA
ROMANIA	17–15	FIJI
FRANCE	19–13	CANADA

THE KNOCKOUT STAGES
QUARTER-FINALS

FRANCE	10–19	ENGLAND
SCOTLAND	28–6	WESTERN SAMOA
IRELAND	18–19	AUSTRALIA
NEW ZEALAND	29–13	CANADA

SEMI-FINALS

SCOTLAND	6–9	ENGLAND
NEW ZEALAND	6–16	AUSTRALIA

THIRD-PLACE MATCH

NEW ZEALAND	13–6	SCOTLAND

THE 1991 WORLD CUP FINAL

ENGLAND	6–12	AUSTRALIA

ENGLAND
J WEBB, S HALLIDAY, W CARLING (CAPT), J GUSCOTT, R UNDERWOOD, R ANDREW, R HILL, J LEONARD, B MOORE, J PROBYN, P .ACKFORD, W DOOLEY, M SKINNER. M TEAGUE, P WINTERBOTTOM

SCORERS
PENS WEBB 2

AUSTRALIA
M ROEBUCK, D CAMPESE, J LITTLE, T HORAN, R EGERTON, M LYNAGH, N FARR-JONES (CAPT), T DALY, P KEARNS, E MCKENZIE, R MCCALL, J EALES, S POIDEVIN, T COKER, V OFAHENGAUE

SCORERS
TRIES DALY   CONS LYNAGH
PENS LYNAGH 2

1991 WORLD CUP RECORDS

MOST POINTS
68 R KEYES (IRELAND), 66 M LYNAGH (AUSTRALIA), 61 G HASTINGS (SCOTLAND)

MOST TRIES
4 B ROBINSON (IRELAND V ZIMBABWE), 3 T WRIGHT (NZ V USA), I TUKALO (SCOTLAND V ZIMBABWE) AND J-B LAFOND (FRANCE V FIJI)

MOST POINTS IN A MATCH
24 J WEBB (ENGLAND V ITALY), 23 R KEYES (IRELAND V ZIMBABWE)

Rainbow nation rises to the occasion

SOUTH AFRICA'S DREAM OF A PLACE IN THE 1995 WORLD CUP FINAL ALMOST ENDED IN RAIN-LASHED KING'S PARK, DURBAN (BOTTOM) WHEN THEY SCRAPED PAST FRANCE 19–15. THE GAME WAS DELAYED 90 MINUTES UNTIL THE DELUGE STOPPED AND WORKERS WERE EVEN FORCED ON TO THE FIELD (BELOW) TO MOP UP THE WATER

South Africa spent more than a decade in the sporting wilderness, banned from competition because of the apartheid regime. So after the boycott was lifted and they returned to international rugby – in 1992 – there was only one place to hold the Rugby World Cup, in the Rainbow Nation.

And they didn't disappoint, with a classic World Cup that captivated not only the continent of Africa but also the whole of the rugby world.

The Springboks were destined to win their own World Cup and after the first final to go into extra time, they triumphed in a pulsating clash with New Zealand.

The All Blacks had blown England away in the semi-finals with an incredible display that announced Jonah Lomu to the world of rugby.

Holders Australia disappeared in the quarter-finals when France once again made the last four. France succumbed to a rampant South African side that seemed to have fate on their side as well as an expectant nation.

THIS WAS THE MOMENT WHEN JOEL STRANSKY SENT A NATION INTO RAPTURES (LEFT) WITH THIS INJURY-TIME DROP GOAL FOR SOUTH AFRICA, AGAINST NEW ZEALAND, WINNING THE 1995 WORLD CUP. THE WEBB ELLIS CUP WAS PRESENTED (RIGHT) BY THE COUNTRY'S PRESIDENT NELSON MANDELA TO THE TEAM'S CAPTAIN FRANÇOIS PIENAAR

SOUTH AFRICA 1995

1995 Stat Attack

The Pool Stages

POOL A

SOUTH AFRICA	27–18	AUSTRALIA
CANADA	34–3	ROMANIA
SOUTH AFRICA	21–8	ROMANIA
AUSTRALIA	27–11	CANADA
AUSTRALIA	42–3	ROMANIA
SOUTH AFRICA	20–0	CANADA

POOL B

WESTERN SAMOA	42–18	ITALY
ENGLAND	24–18	ARGENTINA
WESTERN SAMOA	32–26	ARGENTINA
ENGLAND	27–20	ITALY
ITALY	31–25	ARGENTINA
ENGLAND	44–22	WESTERN SAMOA

POOL C

WALES	57–10	JAPAN
NEW ZEALAND	43–19	IRELAND
IRELAND	50–28	JAPAN
NEW ZEALAND	34–9	WALES
NEW ZEALAND	145–17	JAPAN
IRELAND	24–23	WALES

POOL D

SCOTLAND	89–0	IVORY COAST
FRANCE	38–10	TONGA
FRANCE	54–18	IVORY COAST
SCOTLAND	41–5	TONGA
TONGA 29	29–11	IVORY COAST
FRANCE	22–19	SCOTLAND

THE KNOCKOUT STAGES
QUARTER-FINALS

FRANCE	36–12	IRELAND
SOUTH AFRICA	42–14	WESTERN SAMOA
ENGLAND	25–22	AUSTRALIA
NEW ZEALAND	48–30	SCOTLAND

SEMI-FINALS

SOUTH AFRICA	19–15	FRANCE
NEW ZEALAND	45–29	ENGLAND

THIRD-PLACE MATCH
ENGLAND   9–19   FRANCE

THE 1991 WORLD CUP FINAL
SOUTH AFRICA   15–12   NEW ZEALAND
(AFTER EXTRA TIME)

SOUTH AFRICA
A JOUBERT, J SMALL (B VENTER 97), J MULDER,
H LE ROUX, C WILLIAMS, J STRANSKY, J VAN
DER WESTHUIZEN, O DU RANDT,
P ROSSOUW, B SWART (G PAGEL 68), K WIESE,
H STRYDOM, F PIENAAR (CAPT), M ANDREWS
(R STRAEULI 90), R KRUGER

SCORERS
PENS STRANSKY 3
DROP GOALS STRANSKY 2

NEW ZEALAND
G OSBORNE, J WILSON(M ELLIS 55), F BUNCE,
W LITTLE, J LOMU, A MEHRTENS, G BACHOP,
C DOWD (R LOE 83), S FITZPATRICK (CAPT),
O BROWN, I JONES, R BROOKE, M BREWER
(J JOSEPH 40), Z BROOKE, J KRONFELD

SCORERS
PENS MEHRTENS 3
DROP GOALS MEHRTENS

1995 WORLD CUP RECORDS

MOST POINTS
112 T LACROIX (FRANCE),
104 G HASTINGS (SCOTLAND),
84 A MEHRTENS (NEW ZEALAND)

MOST TRIES
7 M ELLIS (NEW ZEALAND),
J LOMU (NEW ZEALAND)

MOST POINTS IN A MATCH
45 S CULHANE (NEW ZEALAND V JAPAN),
44 G HASTINGS (SCOTLAND V IVORY COAST)

Wallabies hit double top

Australia made rugby history in 1999. Not only did they win the World Cup, but became the first side to lift the Webb Ellis Cup twice, following their triumph at Twickenham in 1991.

This time the celebrations started 200 miles down the M4 in Cardiff as the Millennium Stadium hosted the fourth World Cup final.

Defence was king in 1999 as the Wallabies won rugby's greatest prize in a tournament where they only conceded one try, and that was against the USA in the pool stages, when many of their frontline players were rested.

New Zealand had been everyone's favourites, playing sublime rugby until they met a rampant French side in the semi-final. The All Blacks powered to a 24–10 lead before France staged one of the greatest comebacks in the history of the World Cup to claim the victory.

The French were unable to produce anything like that form in the final as Australia shut down their running game for a comprehensive victory.

GEORGE GREGAN (RIGHT) IS ECSTATIC AFTER AUSTRALIA CLAIMED THEIR SECOND WORLD CUP, WHILE THE WALLABIES AND FRANCE STAND TOE-TO-TOE IN THE FINAL (BELOW)

After a magnificent display through the competition Tim Horan (below) was confirmed as the Player of the Tournament in 1999. "Horan had a wonderful month and not even Jonah Lomu could touch him for contribution to his side's performance," said former Wallabies captain Nick Farr-Jones in Sydney's *Daily Telegraph*. "He invariably found openings in midfield, got over the advantage line and looked to me like he wanted to get his hands on the ball a lot. Two years ago, I admit I thought Tim Horan was washed up and the best years of his rugby career were behind him. Today, he wears the worthy mantle of World Cup player of the tournament."

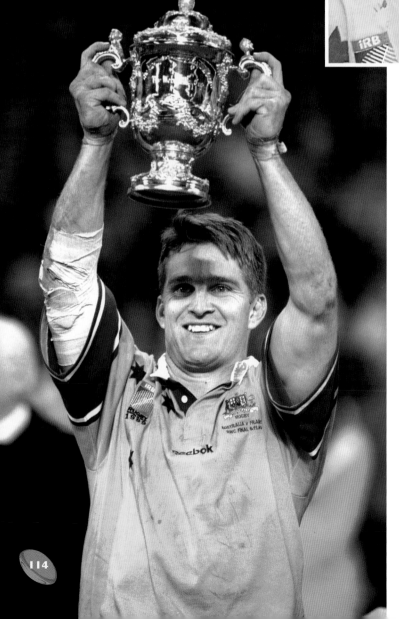

AUSTRALIA WING JOE ROFF GETS THE PARTY STARTED IN THE DRESSING ROOM AFTER THE WALLABIES CLINCHED THEIR SECOND WORLD CUP, FOLLOWING A 35–12 VICTORY OVER FRANCE. THE WIN WAS EARNED AT THE MILLENNIUM STADIUM (RIGHT), OPENED FOR THE 1999 TOURNAMENT

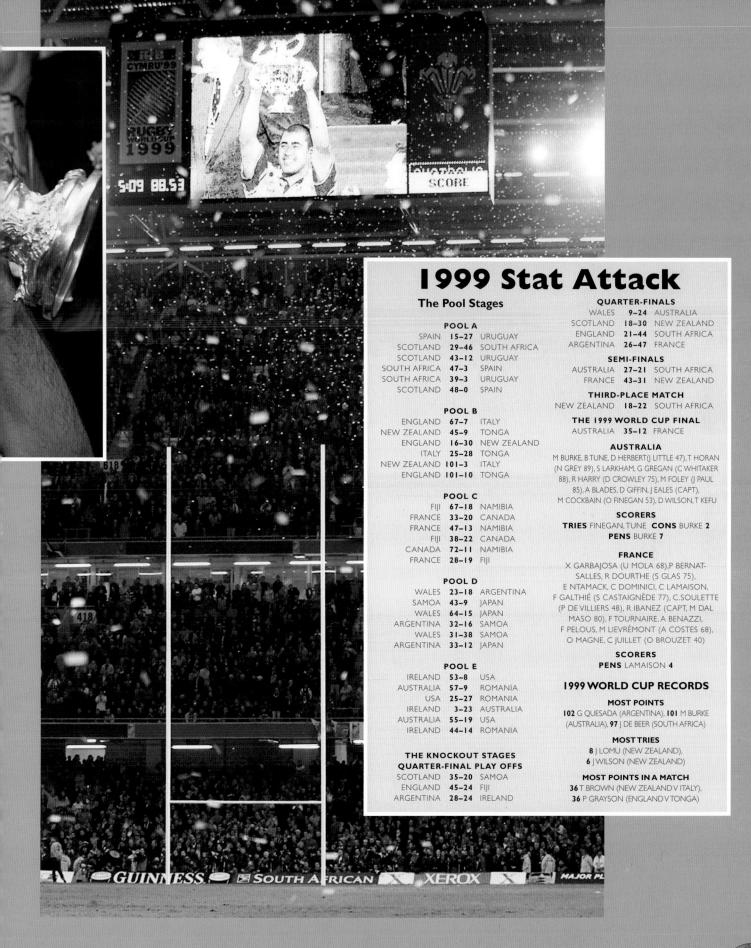

1999 Stat Attack

The Pool Stages

POOL A

SPAIN	15–27	URUGUAY
SCOTLAND	29–46	SOUTH AFRICA
SCOTLAND	43–12	URUGUAY
SOUTH AFRICA	47–3	SPAIN
SOUTH AFRICA	39–3	URUGUAY
SCOTLAND	48–0	SPAIN

POOL B

ENGLAND	67–7	ITALY
NEW ZEALAND	45–9	TONGA
ENGLAND	16–30	NEW ZEALAND
ITALY	25–28	TONGA
NEW ZEALAND	101–3	ITALY
ENGLAND	101–10	TONGA

POOL C

FIJI	67–18	NAMIBIA
FRANCE	33–20	CANADA
FRANCE	47–13	NAMIBIA
FIJI	38–22	CANADA
CANADA	72–11	NAMIBIA
FRANCE	28–19	FIJI

POOL D

WALES	23–18	ARGENTINA
SAMOA	43–9	JAPAN
WALES	64–15	JAPAN
ARGENTINA	32–16	SAMOA
WALES	31–38	SAMOA
ARGENTINA	33–12	JAPAN

POOL E

IRELAND	53–8	USA
AUSTRALIA	57–9	ROMANIA
USA	25–27	ROMANIA
IRELAND	3–23	AUSTRALIA
AUSTRALIA	55–19	USA
IRELAND	44–14	ROMANIA

THE KNOCKOUT STAGES
QUARTER-FINAL PLAY OFFS

SCOTLAND	35–20	SAMOA
ENGLAND	45–24	FIJI
ARGENTINA	28–24	IRELAND

QUARTER-FINALS

WALES	9–24	AUSTRALIA
SCOTLAND	18–30	NEW ZEALAND
ENGLAND	21–44	SOUTH AFRICA
ARGENTINA	26–47	FRANCE

SEMI-FINALS

AUSTRALIA	27–21	SOUTH AFRICA
FRANCE	43–31	NEW ZEALAND

THIRD-PLACE MATCH

NEW ZEALAND	18–22	SOUTH AFRICA

THE 1999 WORLD CUP FINAL

AUSTRALIA	35–12	FRANCE

AUSTRALIA

M BURKE, B TUNE, D HERBERT (J LITTLE 47), T HORAN (N GREY 89), S LARKHAM, G GREGAN (C WHITAKER 88), R HARRY (D CROWLEY 75), M FOLEY (J PAUL 85), A BLADES, D GIFFIN, J EALES (CAPT), M COCKBAIN (O FINEGAN 53), D WILSON, T KEFU

SCORERS
TRIES FINEGAN, TUNE **CONS** BURKE 2
PENS BURKE 7

FRANCE

X GARBAJOSA (U MOLA 68), P BERNAT-SALLES, R DOURTHE (S GLAS 75), E NTAMACK, C DOMINICI, C LAMAISON, F GALTHIÉ (S CASTAIGNÈDE 77), C.SOULETTE (P DE VILLIERS 48), R IBANEZ (CAPT, M DAL MASO 80), F TOURNAIRE, A BENAZZI, F PELOUS, M LIEVRÊMONT (A COSTES 68), O MAGNE, C JUILLET (O BROUZET 40)

SCORERS
PENS LAMAISON 4

1999 WORLD CUP RECORDS

MOST POINTS
102 G QUESADA (ARGENTINA), **101** M BURKE (AUSTRALIA), **97** J DE BEER (SOUTH AFRICA)

MOST TRIES
8 J LOMU (NEW ZEALAND),
6 J WILSON (NEW ZEALAND)

MOST POINTS IN A MATCH
36 T BROWN (NEW ZEALAND V ITALY),
36 P GRAYSON (ENGLAND V TONGA)

Cup heads back to the north

It took until the fifth tournament, but finally a team from the northern hemisphere lifted the Webb Ellis Cup – Clive Woodward's England, led by the indomitable Martin Johnson.

Coming into the tournament as the world's number one team after picking up a Grand Slam earlier in the year, England built up an irresistible momentum that took them through to the World Cup Final.

The final itself – against Australia – was breathtaking.

After the lead changed hands, it was finally settled with just over a minute of extra time to go by a drop goal from Jonny Wilkinson, which sailed through the posts off his weaker right foot.

"It was a huge effort by the entire squad of players, coaches and backroom staff, everybody. Thanks to the fans, they were incredible," said Johnson.

"I can't say enough about the team, because we had the

lead and we lost it but we came back. And I can't say enough about Wilko at the end."

"I'm just so happy for the players, they've put their heart and soul into it. It couldn't have been any closer and I'm just happy I'm on the right side."

Elton Flatley's heroics were almost forgotten in the pandemonium that followed Wilkinson's late kick. After a Lote Tuqiri try took Australia ahead, and England fought back, it was Flatley's boot that tied it up in the second half, to send the game into extra time.

New Zealand once again failed to cope with the pressure of a World Cup. Storming through the pool stages with a mammoth 282 points from four games they faltered in the semi-finals, losing to Australia 22–10. The defeat cost All Blacks coach John Mitchell his job as an unforgiving public turned on the man at the top.

IMANOL HARINORDOQUY FLOATS THROUGH THE AIR FOR A TRY (OPPOSITE BELOW) TO SEND FRANCE THROUGH TO THE WORLD CUP SEMI-FINAL, WHILE (OPPOSITE ABOVE) PHIL VICKERY TURNED HERO WITH A TRY WHEN IT LOOKED AS THOUGH ENGLAND WOULD LOSE TO SAMOA.
(ABOVE) WALES AND ENGLAND BATTLE IT OUT FOR A PLACE IN THE LAST FOUR

Wales showed the green shoots of recovery, pushing both England and New Zealand hard before succumbing in a pulsating quarter-final to England, 28–17.

The rugby world was delighted to see a World Cup debut for the Georgians, but less pleased to see the hammerings dealt to Namibia, Tonga and Romania, which again demonstrated that the gulf between the game's top ten and the rest was growing.

ELTON FLATLEY'S WORLD-CLASS
KICKING PERFORMANCE KEPT
AUSTRALIA IN THE WORLD CUP
FINAL, WITH 12 OF THEIR 17
POINTS. HE WAS ICE COOL WITH
THE BOOT AS AUSTRALIA
CLAWED THEIR WAY BACK IN THE
SECOND HALF (ABOVE). JASON
ROBINSON SCORES ENGLAND'S
ONLY TRY SENDING THEM INTO A
14–5 LEAD (ABOVE RIGHT)

2003 Stat Attack

The Pool Stages

POOL A

AUSTRALIA	24–8	ARGENTINA
IRELAND	45–17	ROMANIA
ARGENTINA	67–14	NAMIBIA
AUSTRALIA	90–8	ROMANIA
IRELAND	64–7	NAMIBIA
ARGENTINA	50–3	ROMANIA
AUSTRALIA	142–0	NAMIBIA
ARGENTINA	15–16	IRELAND
NAMIBIA	7–37	ROMANIA
AUSTRALIA	17–16	IRELAND

POOL B

FRANCE	61–18	FIJI
SCOTLAND	32–11	JAPAN
FIJI	19–18	USA
FRANCE	51–29	JAPAN
SCOTLAND	39–15	USA
FIJI	41–13	JAPAN
FRANCE	51–9	SCOTLAND
JAPAN	26–39	USA
FRANCE	41–14	USA
SCOTLAND	22–20	FIJI

POOL C

SOUTH AFRICA	72–6	URUGUAY
ENGLAND	84–6	GEORGIA
SAMOA	60–13	URUGUAY
SOUTH AFRICA	6–25	ENGLAND
GEORGIA	9–46	SAMOA
SOUTH AFRICA	46–19	GEORGIA
ENGLAND	35–22	SAMOA
GEORGIA	12–24	URUGUAY
SOUTH AFRICA	60–10	SAMOA
ENGLAND	111–13	URUGUAY

POOL D

NEW ZEALAND	70–7	ITALY
WALES	41–10	CANADA
ITALY	36–12	TONGA
NEW ZEALAND	68–6	CANADA
WALES	27–20	TONGA
ITALY	19–14	CANADA
NEW ZEALAND	91–7	TONGA
ITALY	15–27	WALES
CANADA	24–7	TONGA
NEW ZEALAND	53–37	WALES

THE KNOCKOUT STAGES

QUARTER-FINALS

NEW ZEALAND	29–9	SOUTH AFRICA
AUSTRALIA	33–16	SCOTLAND
FRANCE	43–21	IRELAND
ENGLAND	28–17	WALES

SEMI-FINALS

| NEW ZEALAND | 10–22 | AUSTRALIA |
| FRANCE | 7–24 | ENGLAND |

THIRD-PLACE MATCH

| NEW ZEALAND | 40–13 | FRANCE |

THE 2003 WORLD CUP FINAL

| AUSTRALIA | 17–20 | ENGLAND* |

* AFTER EXTRA TIME

AUSTRALIA

M ROGERS (J ROFF), W SAILOR, S MORTLOCK,
E FLATLEY, L TUQIRI, S LARKHAM (M GITEAU),
G GREGAN (CAPT), B YOUNG (M DUNNING),
B CANNON (J PAUL), A BAXTER, J HARRISON,
N SHARPE (D GIFFIN), G SMITH, P WAUGH,
D LYONS (M COCKBAIN)

SCORERS

TRIES TUQIRI **PENS** FLATLEY **4**

ENGLAND

J ROBINSON, J LEWSEY (I BALSHAW),
W GREENWOOD, M TINDALL (M CATT),
B COHEN, J WILKINSON, M DAWSON,
T WOODMAN, S THOMPSON, P VICKERY
(J LEONARD), M JOHNSON (CAPTAIN), B KAY,
R HILL (L MOODY), N BACK, L DALLAGLIO

SCORERS

TRIES ROBINSON **PENS** WILKINSON **4**
DROP GOALS WILKINSON

2003 WORLD CUP RECORDS

MOST POINTS

113 J WILKINSON (ENG),
103 F MICHALAK (FR), **100** E FLATLEY (AUS)

MOST TRIES

7 D HOWLETT (NZ), M MULIAINA (NZ),
6 J ROKOCOKO (NZ), **5** W GREENWOOD
(ENG), C LATHAM (AUS), J LEWSEY (ENG)
M ROGERS (AUS), L TUQIRI (AUS)

BBQ THAT!

JONNY WILKINSON KICKED
THE DROP GOAL THAT
BROUGHT THE WORLD CUP
TO ENGLAND, COMPLETING
A 20–17 VICTORY. AT THE
FINAL WHISTLE BEN
COHEN HUGS WILKINSON
AND LAWRENCE DALLAGLIO
JOINS THE CELEBRATION
(RIGHT) WHILST IN THE
STAND AN ENGLISH FAN
HAS A MESSAGE FOR THE
LOSING SIDE (ABOVE)

PART FOUR
inside the game

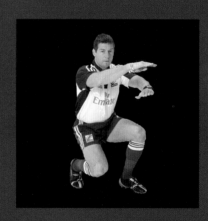

I LONGEST NAME:
Joost van der Westhuizen,
South Africa (below)

**2 FIRST TO PLAY IN
FOUR WORLD CUPS:**
Gareth Rees, Canada
1987–1999

3 MOST CONS:
Gavin Hastings, Scotland 39
(below)

**4 MOST POINTS IN RWC
HISTORY:** Gavin Hastings,
Scotland 227 (above)

6 MOST TRIES:
Jonah Lomu, New Zealand,
15 (below)

7 SHORTEST:
Earl Va'a,
Samoa –
166cm
(right)

**8
THE
LIGHTEST:**
Desmond
Snyders,
Namibia
68Kg

5 HEAVIEST: Joeli Veitayaki, Fiji – 136Kg

9 TALLEST:
Luke Gross,
USA – 206cm
(Left)

... and
Simon Shaw,
England –
206cm
(right)

10 MOST DROP GOALS:
Jonny Wilkinson, England,
8 (below)

Advantage

Ball held up in goal

**Collapsing
Ruck or Maul**

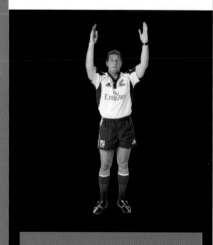

Doctor Needed

Drop out 22

**Failure to
Bind Properly**

Falling over Player

Free Kick

High Tackle

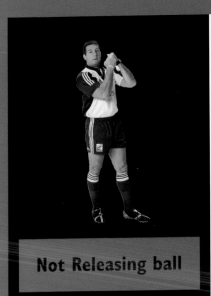

Not Releasing ball

Penalty kick

Punching

Scrum awarded

Stamping

Throw or forward Pass

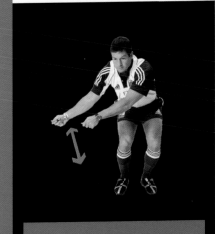

Throw in Scrum Not Straight

Try and penalty

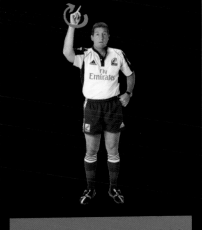

Wheeling Scrum 90° or more

THE INSIDE TRACK

ALL BLACKS The nickname given to the New Zealand team, coined by British newspaper *The Daily Mail* on the 1905 tour.

BACKS Seven of the 15 players in a team are backs. They don't take part in the scrum or lineouts and often score the majority of the tries.

BACK ROW The openside flanker (number seven), blindside flanker (number six) and No 8 make up the back row of the scrum. The most prolific trio – i.e. the back row that has played together in the most internationals – is the England three of Neil Back, Richard Hill and Lawrence Dallaglio, who were together when they won the World Cup in 2003. The presence of the two flankers is one of the key differences between rugby union and rugby league, which has 13 players in each team.

(OPPOSITE) LAWRENCE DALLAGLIO, ENGLAND'S MOST CAPPED BACK ROW FORWARD

BARBARIANS A legendary invitation side which played its first game in 1880, inspired by William Percy Carpmael. Also called the Baa-Baas, they have enjoyed some epic matches down the years, playing all the major club teams and international sides in their famous black and white hoops.

BLINDSIDE FLANKER This player wears number six and he packs down on the blind (or short side) of the scrum. Great exponents include New Zealand's Michael Jones (who was in Rugby World's Team of the Millennium) and England's Richard Hill. Will be expected to put in a huge number of tackles.

CALCUTTA CUP Contested in all matches between England and Scotland, it was made – in the 1870s – from melted down rupees left over when the Calcutta Rugby Club was disbanded.

(RIGHT) SCOTLAND WON THE CALCUTTA CUP IN 2006: CAPTAIN JASON WHITE ACCEPTING THE TROPHY

CENTRE Every great side will have an inside centre (No 12) and an outside centre (No 13) working in perfect harmony. The inside is often the distributor or creator while the outside should be a little quicker. A good inside centre should also be a good kicker out of hand, working with the outside-half. The outside centre needs expert handling and the eye for a gap.

CONVERSION A kick taken after a try and worth two points if the ball is sent over the crossbar.

FORWARDS The eight men entrusted with the prime job of winning the ball. They form the scrum and lineout and will often be around in the rucks and mauls, battling with the opposition.

FULL-BACK The last line of defence, the full-back wears No 15. In the modern game he needs to be as adept in attack as in defence and a reliable kicker out of hand.

GARRYOWEN A high kick, designed to put huge pressure on the opposition, and named after the famous Irish club. Also known as an up and under.

GRAND SLAM A title contested in the Six Nations Championship. A side is said to have completed a Grand

Slam when they beat all other five sides in the Championship, but no trophy is awarded. Wales did a Grand Slam in 2005.

GUINNESS PREMIERSHIP The leading competition in England, the Guinness Premiership is made up of the top 12 teams in the country. Sale Sharks were the champions in 2006. The top four sides in the Guinness Premiership go into a play-off with the final at Twickenham to decide the champions. It was called the Courage League from 1987 to 1997, followed by the Allied Dunbar Premiership and Zurich Premiership, until Guinness took over the sponsorship for the 2005-06 season. Leicester won four successive titles from 1999 to 2003.

HAKA The name given to the war dance or ritual carried out by a number of teams in the rugby world, before a game starts, most notably used by the New Zealand All Blacks. It is used to throw down a challenge to the opposition and is a popular part of the modern game.

HEINEKEN CUP Europe's premier competition, the best sides from England, Ireland, Scotland, Wales, France and Italy contest the Heineken Cup each season. It kicked off in 1996, when it was won by Toulouse. Leicester were the first side to retain the trophy, winning it 15–9 against Munster in 2002.

HOME NATIONS England, Ireland, Scotland and Wales.

HOOKER Standing in the middle of the front row of the scrum, the hooker needs to strong enough to pack down, while he is expected to be a devastating presence around the field and he also throws into the lineout. When there is a scrum they have to 'hook' the ball back when it is fed in by the scrum-half.

IRB The International Rugby Board, the world governing body of the game of rugby union.

(ABOVE) THE LINEOUT HAS BECOME A CRUCIAL PART OF THE GAME

LINEOUT The set piece staged when the ball is kicked out of play. The hooker throws the ball in and the attacking side decides how many players are in the lineout. Anything from four to eight is normal.

MAGNERS LEAGUE The new name for the Celtic League, contested in the UK and Ireland between the best sides in Wales, Scotland and Ireland.

MAUL A ruck when the ball is kept up in the air. A massive battle for the ball with one side trying to march the ball up the field, the other using brute force to stop it.

22-METRE LINE With the rise of the metric system the 20-yard line was abolished. Rugby's equivalent of football's penalty box. If the defensive team kicks the ball in their own 22 the lineout is taken where the ball crosses the line. If they kick it out, from outside their own 22 (except if after a penalty is awarded) the lineout is taken from where they kicked the ball.

OUTSIDE-HALF Rugby's quarterback, the outside-half is the pivot for any team, setting up the back moves. Usually the goalkicker as well, Jonny Wilkinson showed how valuable a great outside-half is in the 2003 World Cup, winning the tournament deep into extra time with a drop goal.

PENALTY Awarded for a number of offences, a side winning a penalty can decide to kick at goal and if the ball is sent through the posts and over the upright it is worth three points.

PROP
Loosehead The loosehead (or number one) props on the left hand side of the scrum, next to where the scrum-half puts the ball into the scrum. One of the unsung heroes, they need huge upper-body strength.
Tighthead The tighthead (or number three) props on the right hand side of the scrum, they are the pillar of strength on which all great packs prosper. Some coaches say when selecting a side you should "pick the tighthead, pick the goalkicker and then pick 13 players to take the field with them" so important is the tighthead to a side.

PROVINCES In Ireland four provinces – Ulster, Munster, Leinster and Connacht – were formed to cover Ireland, both north and south. In the modern game the Irish team is picked from these provinces. In Ireland club sides form the tier below provinces, feeding their players into them.

(BELOW) MUNSTER, THE MEN IN RED, LIFTED THE HEINEKEN CUP IN 2006

RUCK A ruck occurs when the ball is on the ground, normally after a player is tackled. It is formed when two players on their feet, one from each team, arrive at the ball. The referee will often shout 'ruck' to the players when it has been formed as they can no longer put their hands on the ball.

SCRUM-HALF The link between the forwards and the backs, the scrum-half (number nine) needs to be a great passer, organiser, runner and defender, possessing great all-round skills. George Gregan is the most prolific scrum-half in the history of the game, overtaking Jason Leonard's previous record for caps won, in 2005.

SECOND ROW Also referred to as locks, these guys wear four and five and have the key responsibility of winning ball in the lineout. They will be the tallest player on the field, but since the game turned professional they are required to do far more than win lineout ball. Many act as a fourth or fifth back rower, marauding around the field and some like John Eales and Allan Martin have even been known to kick a few goals.

SIN BIN A player who transgresses certain laws is sent to the sin bin for 10 minutes, once the referee has shown the yellow card. The first player to be sent to the sin bin in the World Cup was Manuel Contepomi in 2003.

SIX NATIONS CHAMPIONSHIP The annual competition staged between the test sides of England, Scotland, Wales, Ireland, France and Italy. Won by France in 2006. It was changed from the Five Nations to Six in 2000 when Italy joined.

SPRINGBOKS The nickname given to the South Africa team

SUPER 14 The premier competition in the southern hemisphere, it features the 14 biggest sides (non-international) in New Zealand, South Africa and Australia. It was won by New Zealand's Crusaders (from Canterbury) in 2006 when it was transformed from a Super 12 into a Super 14, two new teams joining the competition. Each side plays 13 games with the top four going into a play-off competition. It was founded in 1996 after rugby turned professional. There are five sides from New Zealand, five from South Africa, with four from Australia in the Super 14. The Auckland Blues won the first two titles.

TRIPLE CROWN In the Six Nations any home nation (Ireland, Wales, Scotland and England) beating all three others is awarded the Triple Crown. Won in 2006 by the Irish.

(ABOVE) IRELAND CAPTAIN BRIAN O'DRISCOLL PROUDLY SHOWS OFF THE 2006 TRIPLE CROWN TROPHY

TRI-NATIONS The annual battle of the three giants of the southern hemisphere; New Zealand, Australia and South Africa, the Tri-Nations kicked off in 1996 after the game turned professional. Dominated in recent years by New Zealand, they won all but one title from 2002 to 2006.

TRY The grounding of the ball over the try line earns five points. Unlike in

(ABOVE) SIMPLY THE BEST ... DAISUKE OHATA, JAPAN'S RECORD BREAKING WING

American football the player in possession must put the ball down and must be in control when he does so.

WALLABIES The nickname given to the Australia team.

WING The quickest players on the field, the right and left wing are the players who score the most tries. It is crucial that a world-class wing is as

good in defence as attack. The leading scorer in Test history is Japan's Daisuke Ohata, who went past David Campese's previous record in 2006.

WOODEN SPOON The title given to the side that finishes bottom of the Six Nations Championship. After England finished bottom in 1983 the Wooden Spoon Charity was formed and since then it has raised millions of pounds supporting mentally, physically and socially disadvantaged children and young people.

Picture credits

Key

t top, m middle, b bottom, l left, r right, i inset

GI Getty Images

AFP Agence France Presse

1 David Rogers/GI; 1il Odd Anderson/AFP; 1ir David Rogers/GI; 2-3 Nick Laham/GI; 2l Cameron Spencer/GI; 2r Nick Laham/GI; 3l Daniel Berehulak/GI; 3r David Rogers/GI; 4 GI; 5t GI; 5b GI; 6 GI; 7t GI; 7b GI; 8t GI; 8b Philip Littleton/AFP; 9 David Rogers/GI; 10-11 Cameron Spencer/GI; 11t Mike Hewitt/GI; 11tm Stu Forster/GI; 11bm David Rogers/GI; 11b David Rogers/GI; 12-13 Daniel Berehulak/GI; 13i David Rogers/GI; 14i Paul Ellis/AFP; 15 Odd Andersen/AFP; 16-17 Odd Andersen/AFP; 16i David Rogers/GI; 17r Odd Andersen/AFP; 18bl David Rogers/GI; 19 David Rogers/GI; 19i David Rogers/GI; 20 Matthew Lewis/GI; 21 Cameron Spencer/GI; 22 Chris McGrath/GI; 23l Damien Meyer/AFP; 23r Cameron Spencer/GI; 24 David Rogers/GI; 25 Phil Walter/GI; 26-7 David Rogers/GI; 27i Mike Hewitt/GI; 28 Jonathan Wood/GI; 29r Nick Laham/GI; 30 Cameron Spencer/GI; 31i Mark Dadswell/GI; 32 Chris McGrath/GI; 33 Bradley Kanaris/GI; 34l Martyn Hayhow/AFP; 35 David Rogers/GI; 36 Mike Hewitt/GI; 37t Jo Caird/GI; 37b Stu Forster/GI; 38t Darren England/GI; 38m Christophe Simon/AFP; 38b Phillipe Lopez/AFP; 39 Odd Andersen/AFP; 40t Toshifumi Kitamura/AFP; 40b Toshifumi Kitamura/AFP; 41tl Jiji Press/AFP; 41tr Chris McGrath/GI; 41b Chris McGrath/GI; 42-3 Stu Forster/GI; 44l Marty Melville/GI; 44r Ross Land/GI; 45t Dean Treml/AFP; 45b Ross Land/GI; 46-7 Dean Treml/AFP; 48-9 Ross Land/GI; 48i Damien Meyer/AFP; 49i Marty Melville/GI; 50i Damien Meyer/AFP; 51 Stu Forster/GI; 52 Jeff J Mitchell/GI; 53t David Rogers/GI; 53b Ian Stewart/AFP; 54l David Rogers/GI; 55t Chris McGrath/GI; 55bl David Rogers/GI; 55br Martin Hayhow/AFP; 56tl Peter Parks/AFP; 56tr Mark Dadswell/GI; 56b Ross Land/GI; 57 Miguel Rojo/AFP; 58-9 David Rogers/GI; 60 Stephane De Sakutin/AFP; 61 Gabriel Bouys/AFP; 62-3 Damien Meyer/AFP; 62i GI; 64 Damien Meyer/AFP; 65r Jamie McDonald/GI; 66 Dean Treml/AFP; 68 David Rogers/GI; 69l David Rogers/GI; 69r David Rogers/GI; 70i Juan Mabromata/AFP; 70bl Ross Land/GI; 71 Patrick Bolger/GI; 72t Peter Parks/AFP; 72b Odd Andersen/AFP; 73t Denis Doyle/GI; 73b Francisco Leong/AFP; 74-5 David Rogers/GI; 76-7 Nick Laham/GI; 76-7 (l-r) Jamie McDonald/GI; Phil Walter/GI; Michael Bradley/GI; Chris McGrath/GI; Damien Meyer/AFP; Damien Meyer/AFP; Mark Nolan/GI; Ryan Pierse/GI; Chris McGrath/GI; David Rogers/GI; Mehdi Fedouach/AFP; Jeff Brass/GI; William West/AFP; Koichi Kamoshida/GI; Stu Forster/GI; Richard Heathcote/GI; 78i Gabriel Bouys/AFP; 78b David Rogers/GI; 79 Phil Walter/GI; 80 Darren England/GI; 81 Dean Purcell/GI; 82l Chris McGrath/GI; 82r Shaun Botterill/GI; 83 Scott Barbour/GI; 84t Ross Land/GI; 84b Lionel Bonaventure/AFP; 85 William West/AFP; 86i Bertrand Langlois/AFP; 87 David Rogers/GI; 88-9 Jon Buckle/GI; 88il Christophe Simon/AFP; 88ir Christophe Simon/AFP; 89il Christophe Simon/AFP; 89ir Christophe Simon/AFP; 90 Phil Walter/GI; 91t Barry Durrant/GI; 91b Ross Land/GI; 92 Gabriel Bouys/AFP; 93tr David Rogers/GI; 93bl Mike Hewitt/GI; 94t Shaun Botterill/GI; 94b David Rogers/GI; 95t Toshifumi Kitamura/AFP; 95b Jiji Press/AFP; 96 Pascal Pavani/AFP; 97it Stu Forster/GI; 97br Mike Hewitt/GI; 98 Michael Steele/GI; 99t Jamie McDonald/GI; 99b David Rogers/GI; 100l GI; 100m GI; 100r David Rogers/GI; 101l Odd Anderson/AFP; 101r David Rogers/GI; 102 Russell Cheyne/GI; 103 Russell Cheyne/GI; 104t Russell Cheyne/GI; 104b GI; 105 Georges Gobet/AFP; 106 Shaun Botterill/GI; 106i GI; 107tr Russell Cheyne/GI; 107ib Shaun Botterill/GI; 108 GI; 109im Simon Bruty/GI; 109b Shaun Botterill/GI; 110it Simon Bruty/GI; 110b Mike Hewitt/GI; 111t Philip Littleton/AFP; 111b Shaun Botterill/GI; 112 Gerry Penny/AFP; 113 William West/AFP; 114t William West/AFP; 114bl David Rogers/GI; 114br Olivier Morin/AFP; 115 Olivier Morin/AFP; 116it Peter Parks/AFP; 116b George Sal/AFP; 117 Darren England/GI; 118tl Odd Anderson/AFP; 118tr Nick Laham/GI; 119tl Phil Walter/GI; 119r Phil Walter/GI; 120t David Rogers/GI; 120m International Rugby Board; 120b Mike Clarke/AFP; 121tl Ross Land/GI; 121tm Olivier Morin/AFP; 121tr Damien Meyer/AFP; 121ml David Rogers/GI; 121m Chris McGrath/GI; 121mr Richard Heathcote/GI; 121bl Damien Meyer/AFP; 121br David Rogers/GI; 122-3 International Rugby Board; 124 Mark Dadswell/GI; 125 Mike Hewitt/GI; 126tl Stu Forster/GI; 126br Stu Forster/GI; 127l David Cannon/GI; 127r Mike Clarke/AFP

This is a Parragon Book

This edition first published in 2007

Parragon Books Ltd
Queen Street House
4 Queen Street
Bath BA1 1HE, UK

Copyright © Parragon Books Ltd 2007
Illustrations copyright © Getty Images 2007

ISBN 978-1-4054-9936-1

This edition created by Endeavour London Limited

Text: Paul Morgan
Design: Paul Welti
Picture research: Paul Morgan
Edited by: Mark Fletcher
Project management: Mary Osborne

Printed in China